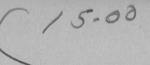

THE WORLD OF GREAT ARCHITECTURE

From the Greeks to the Nineteenth Century

GENERAL EDITOR: BODO CICHY

THE WORLD OF GREAT ARCHITECTURE

From the Greeks to the

Nineteenth Century

R. FURNEAUX JORDAN

112 full page color plates

A STUDIO BOOK

THE VIKING PRESS · NEW YORK

Notes on the plates by Dr Bodo Cichy translated and adapted by C. Ligota

© 1961 THAMES AND HUDSON, LONDON

THIS EDITION OF BAUKUNST IN EUROPA IS

PUBLISHED BY ARRANGEMENT WITH

VERLAGSHAUS ROBERT KOHLHAMMER A.G. STUTTGART

PUBLISHED IN 1961 BY THE VIKING PRESS, INC.

625 MADISON AVENUE, NEW YORK 22, N.Y.

LIBRARY OF CONGRESS CATALOG CARD NUMBER: 61-8828

COLOR PLATES PRINTED IN GERMANY BY CARL RUCK AND HAUFLER & WIEST STUTTGART

TEXT PRINTED IN HOLLAND BY J. H. DE BUSSY

BOUND BY VAN RIJMENAM N.V. THE HAGUE, HOLLAND

CONTENTS

LIST OF PLATES

Plate 1
PAESTUM
Columns of the Basilica

Founded by Greek colonists in 627 BC, Paestum (Poseidonia), like other important towns on the South Italian mainland and in Sicily, has a number of interesting temples. They are all Doric and among the best-preserved examples of the style. As such they make up to a certain extent for the heavy losses suffered by early Doric architecture in the mother country.

The Basilica of Paestum is one of the most significant of these buildings; it is an imposing peripteros (80 × 164 feet) dating from the sixth century and giving a splendid impression of what the archaic stage of Doric was like. Unfortunately all that survives is a part of the colonnade and entablature — enough, however, to give clear indications of an early date: the columns, of varying diameters but all with a tendency to squatness, are closely spaced; the shafts have a pronounced entasis, flat and broad flutings and deeply indented neckings; the echinus is wide and flat and the abacus relatively thick. The direction of subsequent development is clear if this is compared with the classical colonnade of the Temple of Poseidon (mid-fifth century) to be seen in the background of our plate.

Introduction

Architecture is a social art. The painter, the sculptor or poet are all children of their time but they can all at least to some extent withdraw to an ivory tower, there to create according to their whim. Not so the architect. His building may be beautiful, it must be practical. It must provide certain areas of the right size and shape for certain purposes, it must keep out the weather, let in the daylight and endure. That is the least it must do. 'Well

9

building,' said a seventeenth century writer, 'hath three conditions: commodity, firmness and delight', or, as we might say, it must be functional, well-built and pleasing. The story of European architecture is the story of how man, in the designing of cities and buildings, has tried to meet these conditions through some three thousand years of history.

European architecture must obviously, therefore, be an affair of contrasts and variety. Yet, in some mysterious way, for all that

Plate 2
AGRIGENTUM
(ACRAGAS)
The Temple of Castor
and Pollux

The structure illustrated is one corner (restored) of a small late fifth-century temple. The elements of the Doric order are easy to recognise: the classical capital with the underside oblique and almost flat, the deeply incised, thin necking grooves (anuli), and, above, the frieze of metopes and triglyphs, and the geison, the details of which are worthy of particular notice. There are traces of a stucco covering, a common feature of Greek temples, designed not so much to conceal the roughness of the stone and pass it off as marble as to furnish a ground for paint. Greek temples were not originally the masses of naked stone that we know today. Inspired perhaps by the bold colours to be seen on buildings in Egypt, with which there was a lively trade, Greek architects decorated their temples according to strict rules, with red, blue, white and gold as the dominant colours. Even the Parthenon in Athens must once have glowed with colour, traces of which can still be seen.

variety, it is shot through by a single thread, the thread of a common European culture. Violently different in style as are, say, a Greek temple and a Baroque palace, or a Greek temple and a medieval church, they do have something in common — something that they do not share with the architecture of Japan or India. They are different chapters, but different chapters of the same story. The variety and the contrasts derive from the various and contrasting purposes for which buildings have been designed; from the different materials – marble, stone, brick, wood – available in different places; from the different climatic conditions that must be met; above all from changes in method and technique of building such as man's ingenuity devises from time to time.

It is almost a truism to say that architecture reflects society. It does more. It is a most precise indicator of the whole political, economic and cultural world to which it belongs. It is an equally

Plate 2
AGRIGENTUM
(ACRAGAS)
The Temple of Castor
and Pollux

Plate 3
SEGESTA
(EGESTA)
Unfinished Temple

Begun about 420 BC, this Doric peripteros remained unfinished, for the work was interrupted by the Carthaginian invasion of 409. What was erected has been well preserved and presents an interesting 'raw state' casting light on the ancient technique of temple building. For instance the stylobate still has on its vertical face the stone bosses to which ropes were probably tied when the blocks were moved into position and which would normally, once the building was completed, have been cut off. The columns, made up as usual of drums varying considerably in height, are not fluted, an indication that the flutes were carved in columns already standing. Particularly remarkable is the fact that only the columns and the entablature exist and there is no trace of a cella inside. The conclusion to be drawn is that the Greek temple was built from outside to inside, i.e. first columns and entablature and then cella, unless, as has recently been suggested, this temple was not intended to have one.

precise indicator of the geological or climatic region to which it belongs. The great châteaux of the Loire Valley, for instance, with their rounded towers, moats and lavish carving, could have existed only at one moment of history. They belong to the first outburst of the Renaissance in sixteenth century France, when the ghost of the medieval castle was still there to haunt these palaces for the Prince. A generation earlier a castle was just a castle – a stone fort – while a generation later it was a mansion and not a castle at all. Equally, these châteaux could have existed only at one point upon earth, where the earth provided those blue-black slates to cover the steep roofs above walls of gleaming white limestone .... the whole set among the deciduous forests and slow-flowing streams of northern France.

That is a random example. The argument holds good for any building at any time. It is not the whim or desire of the architect that brings about the cathedral, but organised Christendom

Plate 4
DELPHI
The Athenian Treasury

Olympia, to which from 776 BC onwards youths from all parts of Greece came every fourth year to compete in the games, and Delphi, the place of the sacred oracle, were the spiritual centres of the Greek world. They transcended the rivalries of the city-states and fostered a Panhellenic consciousness (awakened politically only after the common struggle for life and death with Persia), of which the treasuries erected in these holy places by each city are as it were the token. They are architectural votive offerings, usually built in the stone of the offering city and intended to house its other contributions. Like our example they were almost all built in the form of the simplest and oldest type of temple, the temple in antis. *This rule holds whatever the style of the details. The lateral walls here project in front of the entrance wall creating a sort of vestibule on whose open side two columns are usually inserted. The type derives from the old Greek megaron which was the model for the earliest temples and whose complicated history can be traced back to the third millennium BC.*

and the craft-guilds, the monastic and feudal systems. Centuries of development in vault-building, masonry and stained-glass were all necessary. And then those high roofs and pinnacled towers are as much a part of the climate and landscape of the grey Gothic North, as the simple marble temple is part of the blue Aegean sea.

European architecture has its roots far back in the story of primitive man, in huts and dolmens and stone circles. It is in

Ancient Egypt that it emerges as a precise craft and a great art. If the pyramids were as useless as they were impressive, they were also among the first monuments in the world to have their stones precisely cut with metal tools, to have their plans precisely drawn, and to be built to accord with the preconception of a master mind. In the Egyptian temples – such as we see at Edfou or Luxor – with their triumphal gateways, colonnaded halls, frescoes and carvings, planning in the grand manner, complicated

Plate 3
SEGESTA
(EGESTA)
Unifinished Temple

Plate 4
DELPHI
The Athenian Treasury

Plate 5
ATHENS
The Parthenon
(View from North-West)

As an unfinished temple of Athena on the Acropolis of her city had been burnt in the Persian Wars, a new one was built between 447 and 438 BC. The architect was Ictinus and the sculptor Phidias, two of the greatest artists of all time. Their work is rightly considered as the most beautiful and perfect achievement of the Doric style. Even though in ruins, the Parthenon demonstrates better than any other temple the character of the Doric style in its fully developed, classical form. Built of marble, the use of which had previously been confined almost entirely to sculpture, it shows that the Doric temple was designed to be a cosmos in itself. The sanctuary (cella) remains hidden behind the peripteral colonnade which surrounds it like a protective wall. The relatively slender shafts of the columns and the elegant articulation of the other elements overcome the almost oppressive heaviness characteristic of earlier Doric temples. But it remains, in spite of the enlivening effect of its sculpture, a compact mass resting on the ground, closed on all sides. There is nothing to indicate the entrance side, to invite the believer to go in, and thus link the outside to the inside. That this effect of an impenetrable solid was consciously intended by the Greek architects is shown by the fact that they sought to enhance it by an optical device: in the Parthenon (and in other temples) not one column has a perpendicular axis. All lean slightly inwards, the corner ones diagonally towards the corners of the cella.

techniques and descriptive art of a high order are united, integrated, for the first time into something we can call 'architecture'. For all that it is really only in Greece of the classical age, about the fifth century BC, that the story of European architecture can be said to begin.

Hand in hand with this compactness goes a wonderful balance between the parts presenting a continuous surface (entablature and pediment) and the open colonnade. Verticals and horizontals, set in stark opposition — the columns against the steps below and the entablature above — hold each other in check. That neither is allowed to dominate and thus disturb the calm of the whole is due primarily to the flat triangular pediment. It rests broadly on the structure underneath and its slowly rising sides take up both directions of movement and resolve the opposition between them in the vertex.

Plate 6
ATHENS
The Temple of
Athena Nike

This elegant structure, erected between 427 and 424 BC on the Athenian Acropolis was dedicated to Nike, the Goddess of Victory. It is amphiprostyle; that is, it has both front and rear porticoes of four columns. The elements of the Ionic order, radically different from the Doric, can be easily appreciated. The slender, very slightly diminishing columns stand on moulded bases which soften the transition from the horizontal, angular substructure of steps to the vertical round supports – an optical effect which in Doric structures would not be tolerated. The flutes are narrower, deeper and more numerous. They do not, as in Doric shafts, meet in sharp arrises but have narrow fillets between them and at the base and capital are joined by semicircular mouldings, thus enhancing the delightful play of light and shadow. The capitals are fully developed Ionic volutes, whose snail-like spirals absorb, as it were, the upward movement in the shafts. There is nothing here of the weight and solidity, nothing of the 'all-sidedness' of the Doric capital. Unequivocally two-sided, and at the angles for aesthetic reasons even three-sided, the Ionic capital has an orientation which not only makes the column itself appear as an individual element, endowed with a definite front, but affects the whole building. The architrave, which rests not on sturdy slabs but on low abaci with curved sides, no longer has the massiveness and puritanical plainness of its Doric equivalent but is enlivened by its three fasciæ, the higher projecting slightly over the lower. As

Greece

The Greek is one of the strangest phenomenon in history. After thousands of years of sprawling fantasy, of oriental tyrants, of monstrous animal-headed gods, of superstition, crudity and darkness, the Greek enters upon the stage of history. The rule of law begins. The great classical age – the Periclean Age in Athens – was short. There was a long and slow preparation through the millennia – Ancient Egypt, Mesopotamia, Troy, the Aegean

for the frieze, the harsh alternation of triglyph and metope is replaced by an elegant continuous relief with figures — a typically Ionic feature for which in other Ionic structures a plain frieze is sometimes substituted. Further up there is a finely moulded, partly preserved geison which was probably surmounted by a pediment with figures.

empire of Cretan kings, the warlords of the Greek mainland. Then, in the fifth century BC, the Greek, more particularly the Athenian, came into his own. Our own law and drama, our poetry and architecture, our philosophy and hygiene were all born. After that — with the return of the tyrant in Alexander the Great and Philip of Macedon, with Magna Graecia and the emergence of Rome — the decadence and then the decline set in. Classical Greece was the perihelion of a comet.... a long approach, a brief blaze

Plate 5
ATHENS
The Parthenon
(View from North-West)

Plate 6
ATHENS
The Temple of
Athena Nike

of light, and then a long dying fall. But in the light of the brief blaze we are living still.

Like all great people the Greek was of mixed race. He himself believed, with some truth, that he was a balance between the Dorian and the Ionian, and these names he perpetuated in two styles of temple building – Doric and Ionic – as we see them on the Acropolis at Athens. The Dorian tribes were probably a hardy people, shepherds from the northern steppes, bringing with

33

them Spartan continence, restraint and courage. The Ionians were a warmer, more effeminate, luxurious and glamorous people from Asia Minor. They brought grace and colour to offset the dour strength of Doric art.

Greece is a small country, a peninsular with many islands and a ragged coastline. The Greeks were a sea-faring people, importing and exporting around the shores of the Eastern Mediterranean and the Black Sea, but penetrating into the mainland of Europe

34

Plate 8
ATHENS
The Temple of
Olympian Zeus

The temple of Olympian Zeus in Athens was begun about 530 BC by the tyrant Pisistratus. Inspired by the vast polystyle sanctuaries of the Greek cities in Asia Minor, it was to be an Ionic dipteros (tripteral at the ends) of gigantic dimensions (157×354 feet). But the building was interrupted after having got no further than the substructure of steps, and it was not resumed until the Late Hellenistic period when, in 174 BC, Antiochius IV of Syria had it built on the original foundations and to the original plan. Its completion was delayed until the reign of Hadrian (AD 117–138). Of this second largest of all Greek temples there have survived parts of the architrave and fifteen of the original hundred and four massive columns, over fifty-five feet tall. Their acanthus leaf capitals, each taller than a man, belong to the latest of the three orders of ancient architecture, the Corinthian. From the third century onwards the order had gradually replaced its two predecessors, the Doric and the Ionic, in the various Hellenistic states of Asia Minor that had sprung from the Empire of Alexander the Great. It was now spreading all over the Mediterranean and appeared also in Athens.

As the remains of the Olympieum show, the Corinthian order is largely a continuation of the Ionic except for the capital. The numerous columns, the wide spaces between them, the threefold

and Africa hardly at all .... merchants and sailors but not empire builders. Love of the sea is redolent in their poetry – 'the wine-dark sea' – and in the wind-blown draperies of their sculpture. Sometimes they set their temples on headlands. Deep inlets of the ocean, as well as mountains, divided city from city, so that Greece, in our sense of the word, was hardly a nation at all. The cities might sometimes, as in the Persian Wars, band together, but it was the City, the Polis, rather than Hellas, that mattered.

35

stepping of the architrave – all this is an Ionic legacy. The only
other innovations are the square slabs (plinths) under the bases of
the columns.

The Greek was proud of his Hellenism – non-Hellenic peoples
were barbarians – but he was prouder still of being a Spartan,
a Corinthian or an Athenian. It was in his loyalty to his city
and in his love of nature that the Greek found expression for
his democracy, his religion, his art and his architecture.

It is in just these things that we find also the limitations of
the Greek. He may have set up the laws in the market place but
his democracy was not our democracy. It was limited to the

Plate 7
ATHENS
The Erechtheum,
Porch of the Maidens

Plate 8

ATHENS

The Temple of
Olympian Zeus

Plate 9
ROME
The Temple of
Antoninus and Faustina

Like many other works of Roman Antiquity that have come down to us, this well preserved temple on the Forum at Rome owes its survival to the fact that it was early converted into a Christian church (San Lorenzo in Miranda). Its architecture and its original purpose are equally instructive. The fundamental differences between the Greek and the Roman temple are here clearly demonstrated. The Greek peripteros is directionless, treated identically on all sides and has its spiritual centre within itself. What we have before us, on the other hand, is a clearly orientated building. An elongated rectangle in plan and without enclosing columns, it stands on a high podium which is of Etruscan derivation, as is the deep porch in front of the entrance wall (altered in the Baroque). The podium is approached by an open flight of steps on which remains of the sacrificial altar have been preserved. The steps and the unfluted, monolithic, fifty-five feet tall Corinthian columns of the porch give a pronounced emphasis to the entrance side, thus imparting a clear direction to the whole structure and relating it to the outside world. Antoninus Pius, the predecessor of Marcus Aurelius, had the temple erected in memory of his consort, the elder Faustina, who died in AD 141. The inscription, DIVAE FAUSTINAE EX S.C., cut on the architrave, in a typically Roman manner, indicates that it was intended primarily not as a sanctuary in the strict sense but, like many other Roman temples, as a memorial to someone whose rank or merit on earth

male Hellene and so was in effect a democracy of a single orator's audience – a city democracy. And in religion, if the Greek had gone beyond the monster-gods of primitive man it was not as yet to the idea of a single God the Father, nor even to the wrathful Jehovah of the Jews. Greek religion was a deification of the powers of nature, of virtues and of the city. Athene was goddess of wisdom as well as of Athens – born miraculously, fully-armed from the head of Zeus. It is important to remember too that

41

entitled her to divine honours. This reflects the Roman attitude towards gods and men, radically different from that of the Greeks: a pronounced cult of the individual, and the importance attached to one's own posthumous fame. When Antoninus died in AD 161, the temple was made to serve his cult too, and the additional inscription was cut on the frieze, directly above that of Faustina: DIVO ANTONINO ET ...

these deities were conceived as physically perfect men and women. The Greek love of beauty found its highest achievement in an understanding of the human form, of anatomy, and the representation of that form in drawing and sculpture. We see here immediately a close link between the Olympic games – where the athletes were naked – and religion and art. There was the danger of course that this monosexual society could enter all too easily upon decadence, but in the classical age these things were

Plate 10
ROME
Circular Temple
by the Tiber

For their smaller temples the Romans occasionally adopted the tholos, developed by the Greeks in the fourth century and consisting of a round cella within a circular peripteros. This elegant, well preserved structure on what used to be the cattle-market (Forum Boarium) in Rome, confused for a long time with the celebrated and highly revered Temple of Vesta, is a fine and characteristic example of the type. The base, though low, is a Roman podium rather than a Greek crepis because the steps leading up to it do not run all round but form a flight of limited width. But the wish to remain close to Greek models is evident in the fine working of the columns, the use of marble and the general disposition of the building. On the strength of these and other features the Temple can be dated to the late Republic or early Empire (second half of first century BC), a period noted for its Philhellenism in art and also for the presence of numerous Greek artists in Rome. The entablature is unfortunately lost, and the wonderful Corinthian capitals crowning the twenty columns are not original but were transferred from another structure when the decaying temple was converted into a church.

The treatment of the ashlars in the wall of the cella is worth noting: they do not form a uniform, smooth surface as in Greek buildings but, in a typically Roman manner, are depressed at the edges, the resulting pattern of wide surfaces and narrow strips giving the wall a varied, painterly appearance.

all manifestations of a worship of the human body, sensuous but pure. This may also explain why the Greek temple – though a fascinating structure – was primarily a vehicle for a sculpture concerned wholly with the outward form of men.

The Greek then – at least in the great Periclean age – was self-absorbed, obsessed with his own conduct – 'know thyself' – 'nothing too much' – with the ideal of the perfectly balanced man, and with the ideal of the perfectly balanced work of art,

43

from which you can take nothing and to which you can add nothing. He was obsessed too with the good city and with public works. That city and its architecture expressed both his ideals and his limitations. The sea-faring Greek was no empire builder. His few colonies were only trading posts. His laws were meant to make his own life tolerable; they were not something to be imposed upon other peoples. True, it was Greek and Phoenician trading that eventually brought a Mediterranean world into

Plate 10
ROME
Circular Temple
by the Tiber

Plate 11
ROME
The Pantheon

This remarkably well-preserved temple fully deserves its reputation as one of the boldest architectural achievements of all time. Its dome, the largest produced in Antiquity, demonstrates the skill of the Romans in vaulting, a skill all their own and not inherited from the Greeks to whom it was almost unknown.

The meaning of the name Pantheon *was uncertain already in Antiquity but it seems likely that the temple was intended for the worship not of one but of several deities, among them the seven planets.*

Of the original structure, begun in 27 BC by Marcus Agrippa, Augustus' son-in-law, little has remained. It was burned down to the foundations in AD 80, and what we see today is a restoration dating from Hadrian's time, built between AD 120 and AD 130. The Pantheon marks an important stage in the development of sacred architecture in its shift of emphasis, in terms of decorative display, from the exterior, remarkably sober and simple, to the interior which, even in its present state of deprivation, can suggest the splendour of its original ornament. This 'interiorisation' will become more and pronounced until it comes fully into its own in the Christian basilica of the fourth century.

The layout of the interior is amongst the finest we know; Michelangelo spoke of it as the production of an angel not of a man.

being, but at that point the Greek had to hand on the torch to the coarser, more efficient Roman – the road-builder, administrator and engineer. Rome was a capital whence an empire could be ruled, not so Athens. Rome, as a capital, was to need many types of building for many purposes. They necessitated complex structure, engineering far beyond the Greek mind. Rome – with its squares and streets and triumphal avenues – had to be planned in the grand manner, an expression of imperial majesty . . . . not

49

The vast rotunda is pervaded by a calm of ineffable solemnity, due as much to its directionless circularity as to its harmonious proportions. Height and diameter correspond exactly – just under 143 feet each. Similarly dome and substructure – each approximately 91 feet high. The overall effect is enhanced by the ingenious simplicity of the lighting: the fabric is pierced nowhere except at the top of the dome where a gigantic circular opening (oculus) admits a stream of sunlight which is evenly distributed over the walls of the interior but focussed, according to the time of day, on one of the seven niches which originally housed statues of gods, possibly the planetary deities. We must imagine the light scintillating on the gilt bronze surface of the coffers in the vault, playing on the coloured marble veneer of the walls of the substructure, and bringing out of the shadow of their niches the marble statues of the gods.

so the city of Athens.

Athens, for all its glories, was a very simple city. It was built not as Rome was, for all the world to see, but for the Athenian. The Greek house, architecturally speaking, hardly existed. It was much like other houses – then or since – in any city of the Eastern Mediterranean. It was flat-roofed, whitewashed and inward looking, with seclusion for women and with the windows onto a small inner court. Streets, apart from the colonnaded Agora or

Plate 12
ROME
The Colosseum

The proverbial demand of the Roman populace for games as well as for bread, whatever we may think of its morality, cannot be denied the merit of having called forth new and grandiose feats in architecture. In Rome and in the provinces, in Britain and Gaul as well as in Africa, is was almost a public duty to hold murderous exhibition fights and pageants of all kinds, and consequently to provide an architectural setting for their performance.

It was the amphitheatre as against the theatre and the race-course that witnessed the worst excesses – gladiatorial contests, animal-baiting and the slaying of Christians. Remains of seventy amphitheatres have survived; the most magnificent of them is undoubtedly the Flavian Amphitheatre in Rome, solemnly inaugurated by Titus in AD 80, and later known as the Colosseum from the colossal column standing nearby which had originally carried a statue of Nero. Although today the vast structure is in ruins, having been in later centuries deprived of its marble facing, partly dismantled and used as a quarry, the impression it makes is still overwhelming.

Like other amphitheatres, the Colosseum consisted of an oval stage, the arena, in the centre, round which rose tiers of seats faced with marble capable of accommodating about 60,000 and divided into three portions designed for the nobility, the free citizens and the plebs. An elaborate system of gangways and steps connected the various levels and led to the seats. The enclosing wall, partly

market-place, were only alleys. Upon this simple, labyrinthine city there looked down the great rock of the Acropolis. It was upon the buildings that he set high on this rock, rather than upon the town itself, that the Greek lavished his genius. It was there that he placed his temples. These were the public works built under Pericles, partly to replace earlier but cruder buildings that had been burnt. There, on the Acropolis, stood the Erechtheum *(plate 7)*, the delicate, richly carved Ionic temple dedicated to

51

preserved, was originally three-storeyed, a fourth storey being added
subsequently. 573 yards in circumference and 159 feet high, it is a
prize example of the Roman treatment of the outer shell of a vast
open air structure: tiers of round arches on pillars framed by semi-
engaged columns, separated from each other by sturdy friezes. The
system is a combination of the Roman round arch as developed in
aqueducts and bridges, and the Greek column-and-architrave, here
transformed into a purely ornamental motif. The sequence of the
Greek orders from the ground upwards – Doric, Ionic and Corinthian
(in the upper storeys they have typically Roman high pedestals) –
shows that their aesthetic significance and possibly their historical
succession were still appreciated. The later fourth storey was a solid
wall; the consoles projecting between its Corinthian pilasters served
to secure the wooden masts planted in special openings in the cornice,
to carry ropes on which were hung awnings for the protection of the
audience from the sun.

the most venerable of all the gods, to Erechtheus. There stood the
Propylaea – not properly a temple but rather a columned gateway
leading to the whole Acropolis enclosure. Alongside the Propylaea was the tiny temple of the Wingless Victory, Nike Apteros
(plate 6) – a foil to the larger buildings. Then there was, finally,
the Parthenon – the large and simple Doric temple of the goddess
Athene herself.

These temples were shrines, not churches. They were not for

Plate 11
ROME
The Pantheon

Plate 12
ROME
The Colosseum

Plate 13
ROME
The Basilica of Maxentius

The many and various tasks arising out of the administration of the Roman Empire, with its world-wide trade and its predominantly urban culture, tended to make public life more important than religion. Not surprisingly, the fact was reflected in Roman architecture. From an early date, beginning naturally in Rome itself, public buildings equalled or surpassed sacred ones in size and magnificence, providing an appropriate setting for the official appearance of republican magistrates and later of emperors. They clustered round the Forum or were part of imperial palaces. The type of building adopted at least from late Republican times (first century BC) onwards was the basilica, a fact of decisive importance for the subsequent history of Christian church architecture. Its chief significance for the future was in its layout: a rectangle divided into a central portion with aisles either all round or (not so often) on the long sides only, the central portion being a storey higher with windows in the upper walls. On one of the narrow sides was a podium or else a semi-circular, vaulted exedra (apse) in which the praetor might administer justice or the emperor take his seat in state.

Unfortunately, of most Roman basilicas only the barest traces have remained. The latest and the most imposing ancient structure of this type, begun by Maxentius just off the Forum in AD 306 and completed by his victorious adversary Constantine, soon after AD 312, has also been reduced to ruin. Known alternately by the names of

congregation; the ordinary citizen seldom entered them – to him their power was the power of a mystery. The Parthenon was simply the shrine of Athene, a house for her gold and ivory statue. Indeed, archaeologically it can be shown that the temples were but heightened or sublimated versions in marble of the archaic timber houses of the war-lords. Such sacred marble shrines were, however, appropriately set apart on the Acropolis, away from the everyday life of the streets. Yet they were always visible

its two imperial patrons, the gigantic edifice covered a surface into which Cologne Cathedral would fit comfortably (328×213 feet). It had the characteristic basilican layout and the higher central portion stretching from the entrance to the projecting apse was spanned by three powerful groin vaults probably modelled on those of the Thermae of Caracalla and Diocletian. Richly-coffered transverse barrel vaults over the lateral aisles and buttresses on the roofs above took the thrust of the central vault; this no longer survives but its springing can still be seen between the arches (see plate). The Basilica of Maxentius was thus a magnificent example of the highly developed vaulting technique of the Romans and of the proficiency they had attained in tackling complicated problems of statics.

from the streets – a reminder of unseen but beneficient powers.

All this was taken account of in the architecture itself. The Parthenon, for instance, *(plate 5)* is basically a very simple building designed not only to be seen from close to by those on the Acropolis, but also to be seen from far off. It had to 'read' when seen from the streets of Athens. In essence – though there were many variations upon the theme – the Greek temple was just a plain rectangular hall – the shrine – surrounded by a colonnade

58

Plate *14*
ROME
The Arch of Septimius
Severus

The desire of the Romans to give due recognition to great deeds and to hold them up as examples to posterity contributed to one of the most distinguished creations of ancient architecture – the triumphal arch. Since the middle Republic (about 200 BC) the practice had grown of erecting arches in honour of victorious generals and of other citizens who had had deserved well of the fatherland. We do not know what they looked like because they were probably temporary wooden structures designed to be dismantled after the day of triumph. They may originally have been connected with the ancient rite of purification by passage through a consecrated 'strait'. In the case of a victorious army, marching through a triumphal gate would deliver it of the pollution with enemy blood. However under the Empire, triumphal arches were of stone or marble and the dominant idea was that of a lasting memorial to the men in whose honour they was erected. The oldest extant arch in Rome is a good example as it was dedicated by the Senate and People to the Emperor Titus after his death. Other arches, erected in various parts of the Roman Empire – about one hundred are known – are probably to be understood in the same terms.

The arch illustrated was put up in honour of Septimius Severus on the Forum Romanum in AD 203. The Emperor had returned in the previous year from his Eastern campaigns, particularly against the Parthians, and a stylised version of his exploits is recorded on the

– the peristyle. In the case of the Parthenon the simple, almost unadorned Doric columns alternating with the broader bands of shadow between them – and we must remember the strong sunlight – gave just the right degree of boldness for the distant view. An intricate building would have been wrong.

Structurally too the building was simplicity itself. It probably had a timber roof covered with marble tiles, and the peristyle, while complex in detail, is essentially no more than a series of

arch in word and image – in the inscription occupying the whole of the attica, and in the reliefs arranged in superimposed registers above the side passages. In the spandrels above the higher middle arch fly victories; the whole was originally crowned by a chariot with eight horses in gilt bronze carrying a statue of the victorious Emperor made of the same material.

Structurally the monument is significant in that it offers again the typical combination of the Roman arch with the Greek column-and-architrave. As in the Colosseum, the latter element has no structural function, being applied to the surface of the fabric in a purely decorative way. There are other distinctly Roman features: the slender free-standing columns are carried on high pedestals with relief decoration; the capitals are of the composite type evolved by the Romans in the first century after Christ from the Ionic and the Corinthian; the richly moulded and ornamented frieze projects over the columns – this last, together with the general tendency to ornamental richness, crowd-scenes in the reliefs and variegated effects of light and shadow, is indicative of a tendency towards picturesqueness in Roman architecture at the turn of the second to third century.

stone lintels on stone pillars. Structurally this takes us no further than Ancient Egypt or Stonehenge. It is only when we climb the Acropolis, pass through the Propylaea, and approach nearer that we find how deceptive is this simplicity. The Greeks may not have been engineers; they were certainly sculptors. The Parthenon was indeed conceived almost as sculpture. It has been said that if the architect could have carved it out of a single gigantic block of marble he would have done so.

Plate 13
ROME
The Basilica of Maxentius

Plate 14
ROME
The Arch of Septimius
Severus

Plate 15
ROME
The Mausoleum of
Hadrian,
Castel Sant' Angelo

To the Romans the appeal of posthumous fame must have been almost magical. True, it was not the fortune of everyone to be a successful general or perform other glorious deeds entitling him to a triumphal arch, a column, or some similar monument. But there was another way of ensuring one's enduring presence in the memory of others: the monumental tomb. Every Roman citizen had the right to build himself one and as nothing was laid down regarding the shape and size of such structures, the law enjoining no more than that cremated remains (inhumation came in only gradually, in the late Empire) should be laid to rest extra muros, *private taste could be freely indulged and 'appropriate' monuments erected if not according to merit at least according to means. The Romans took full advantage of this right and the Via Appia Antica, for instance, is lined for miles on end with a wonderful variety of tombs: simple steles with epitaph and portrait of the deceased, commemorative columns, temple-like edifices, and the gigantic circular mass of the tomb of Caecilia Metella. Nothing was too fanciful: the praetor Caestius played the Pharaoh and built himself a pyramid while the master baker Eurysaces, conscious of the dignity of his profession, designed his tomb in the shape of an old Roman baking oven.*

This bewildering diversity should not, however, be allowed to obscure the fact that most sepulchral monuments followed the old

The sculpture is most closely integrated with the building. Sculpture and architecture are one. The sculpture is designed not only for its place in the building but also for its distance from the eye of the beholder. Seeing that sculpture now, as the Elgin Marbles in the British Museum, we can hardly appreciate this. It is most important if we are to understand the architecture. The whole scheme of the sculpture is in four movements. The figures in the pediment – the low-pitched gable – were in the round and

65

Italic and Etruscan tradition of the funerary chamber inside a tumulus. When the first emperor, Augustus, had a mausoleum built for himself and his family (in 28 BC), the edifice whose imposing remains can be seen next to the Ara Pacis, it was designed basically as an Etruscan tumulus: a round substructure with the funerary chamber in the centre and a conical stone top covered with earth.

The tumulus type is perhaps at its most grandiose in the mausoleum of Hadrian on the right bank of the Tiber, began in AD 135. It has come down to us in a considerably altered form as the Castel Sant' Angelo. Transformed into a fortress as early as AD 275, and subsequently often used as such, it underwent many further alterations, and all that recalls its original appearance is the sturdy drum or round tower (70 yards in diameter) and the high square substructure (length of side: 92 yards). The facing of Parian marble and the colonnade that encircled the drum, as well as the mound at the top which carried an aedicule, probably crowned by a quadriga of gilt bronze, are all completely lost.

were more than life-size. This pediment sculpture, like the peristyle, was bold in design, with bold shadows, and was intended to be seen from far off. That was the first movement. Then, as one got closer, one saw the frieze above the columns – alternate panels of sculpture and almost plain blocks – running right round the temple. Intended to be seen from, at most, about fifty yards away – i.e. from on the Acropolis itself – these panels (metopes) contained figures rather less than life-size. They were not in the

Plate 16
SEGOVIA
Aqueduct

For their temples, theatres, palaces etc. the Romans drew largely on their Etruscan heritage or else learnt diligently, though by no means slavishly, from the Greeks. But in their vast engineering works – roads, bridges and aqueducts – they had to be original. Their tendency to 'rule over nations', their virtus *that triumphed over difficulties, and their practical and purposeful turn of mind served them in good stead. The round arch which the Etruscans had used occasionally offered the means for surmounting natural obstacles such as river and valley with bold constructions in stone. This determination to dominate nature led to constructional feats which, even though severely practical and having no aesthetic intention, are impressive in their bold conception and also important for their influence on more 'artistic' architecture (compare the Colosseum, plate 12).*

The earliest and also the largest arched structures were put up for aqueducts which supplied water, often over considerable distances, to the many wells and bathing establishments of the populous Roman towns. This frequently involved negotiating difficult ground and, as our pump system was not known, the channels, sometimes over six miles long, had to be given a slight slope downwards. Aqueducts were constructed all over the Empire, and that built at Segovia in Spain at the beginning of our era is a fine example. 894 yards long, its two storeys of arches rise to 183 feet. The channel itself is

round but were still in fairly high relief to give bold shadows. That was the second movement.

Now one arrives under the portico or peristyle. One looks up, and there – intended to be seen only now – is the second frieze, the famous band of carving around the wall of the shrine itself. This is in very low relief. This accords both with the nearness of the observer and with the fact that the frieze, being part of the wall is also part of the structure, and so must not be deeply cut.

67

hollowed out in the course of masonry at the top. Though a soberly practical structure, the aqueduct is not without a certain aesthetic appeal created by the rapid succession of the narrow arched openings.

This frieze represents the youths and maidens and horsemen of Athens in procession to present Athene with her new robe – an event which actually took place each year. The procession moves round both sides of the temple towards a group of Olympian gods. They are seated in easy converse over the western door – some of the loveliest figures ever carved. That frieze is the third movement. The fourth and culminating one is the actual statue of Athene within the shrine.

Plate 15
ROME
The Mausoleum of
Hadrian,
Castel Sant' Angelo

Plate 16
SEGOVIA
Aqueduct

Plate *17*
NIMES
Pont du Gard

The most imposing and beautiful of Roman aqueducts is the Pont du Gard, built in the early first century after Christ near the small South French town of Nîmes. It was designed to serve as both bridge and aqueduct, which accounts for its name. Over the lower range of arches which cross the river in wide spans and whose piers are reinforced on their upstream faces with cut-waters, runs a road at the side of which stand the sturdy piers carrying the higher range of arches. At the top, bringing the total height to nearly 162 feet, is a low third storey with numerous smaller arched openings, in the body of which runs the channel.

As in Segovia one is again struck by the sweep and boldness of the engineering performance. It is undoubtedly in constructions of this type that the Romans acquired the knowledge that enabled them to use the vault to such astonishing effect in their temples (e.g. the Pantheon), baths and basilicas.

So much for the actual sculpture .... but the building itself is also virtually sculpture. It is not in fact, when one comes to analyse it, merely a row of cylindrical columns around a central hall. It is more than that. It is, for instance, based on a series of related proportions – rather as an ideal human figure might be. The diameter of the column at its base is a kind of unit or 'module' from which the whole temple can be built up. The column itself is so many diameters high, and so with all the other parts of the temple. In the Parthenon there are no straight lines. Every so-called horizontal line is curved very slightly upwards to avoid all effect of sagging or weakness. The column has an 'entasis' – that is it has in silhouette not only a taper but a slight bulge – again to avoid the weakness of the opposite effect. All the columns tip fractionally inwards. And so it runs, according to a complicated mathematical system, throughout the temple. These proportions gave unity to the Parthenon; these refinements

74

Plate *18*
TRIER
Porta Nigra

The political insecurity which undermined life and thought in all parts of the Roman Empire in the course of the third century, and from which even Rome itself did not escape, increased the need to fortify not only towns and military strong points on the threatened limes but also important localities within the Empire. Rome, until then an open city, had a wall 12 miles long thrown round her by Aurelian and Probus (begun in AD 271).

Though art no longer flourished and had largely exchanged its former splendour for a provincial coarseness, its failing energy found some scope in the gates of town fortifications. The finest example is without doubt the Porta Nigra, so called on account of its blackened stone. It was erected probably in the early fourth century, under Constantine, as part of the ring of fortifications enclosing the town which in AD 287 had become the imperial residence in the West. Intended with its two passages for two-way traffic, the gate consisted of a central square court originally uncovered, flanked by two rectangular towers with semicircular projections on the side away from the town, and connected by galleries at two levels. Particularly interesting is the articulation of the façade: its round arches on piers and the system of 'blind' column-and-architrave recall, if in a provincially simplified version, first century practice in Rome – (e.g. the Colosseum plate 12). However, while the upper storeys were pierced with openings, the substructure of the towers,

stamped it as a building both of grace and strength. The refinements were mathematically minute; to what extent they really corrected optical illusions and to what extent they gave philosophical satisfaction, we shall never know. The Greek was a great mathematician, but mathematics had for him a mystical rather than a practical value.

What all this meant in terms of careful drawing, accurate setting out and skilled marble cutting – the whole thing was built with

75

as the most vulnerable part, remained solidly closed behind the
engaged colonnade.

hair joints – may be imagined. It was marble, but it was also what a modern engineer would call a 'precision' building. Age has made this Penthelic marble honey-coloured, but to envisage a new Parthenon as gleaming white may be misleading. To what extent it was painted, even enamelled, we shall never know. The figures in the sculpture were certainly coloured naturalistically; possibly the mouldings, columns and even walls were coloured too. Paint has been found only in a few crevices. If the Parthenaic

Plate 17
NIMES
Pont du Gard

Plate 18
TRIER

Porta Nigra

Plate 19
ROME
Santa Sabina

The Church of Santa Sabina, a basilica built on the Aventine about AD 425 has preserved its original appearance better than most other early Christian churches. The exterior is remarkably sober and simple – no ornament to arrest the eye, no structural variation to modify the compactness of the uniform mass of masonry. There are only bare, unattractive surfaces of brick as though the structure had been left unfinished – a mistaken impression because this bleakness had a deeper meaning: it was intended as a deliberate contrast with the transfigured world of the interior whose decorative splendour was a sign of the reality of the worshipper's experience. Although the original ornamentation has suffered severely, the walls of the nave for instance, having lost their mosaics and marble veneer almost completely, the transition from outside to inside remains impressive. The interior has preserved a dignified, restrained solemnity and the sweep of the structural conception can still be appreciated. The articulation of space in the basilica at once symbolises and enforces the way to God who is present on the altar in the semicircular apse. Every structural element is utilised to direct the eye towards this point: the rapid succession of supports, wonderful Corinthian columns from an ancient Temple of Juno, the series of round arches, the uniform courses of the upper walls, the rows of windows and finally the large surfaces of the floor and the wooden ceiling.

essence shows, on the one hand, the restraint and refinement of the Greek mind, it is possible that, on the other hand, its gaudy colouring would have shown us that even classical Greece was part of the Mediterranean world of her day .... only a generation removed from barbarism.

The Parthenon – as one example of the many temples that the Greeks built – has here been described rather fully. It came at the end of a long process. It had emerged from a dark and fearful

past. It was derived from the wooden houses of primoeval chieftains, as well as from crude and archaic stone temples *(plates 1,
2 and 3)*. It was, however, also the beginning of something – of
European architecture. It was a seminal building. To its well-
ordered plan, to its craftsmanship, unity and precision, our architecture – whatever its style – owes much.

Plate 20
RAVENNA
Sant' Apollinare in Classe

This basilica was built between AD 534 and 549 in Classis, once the port of Ravenna. It has survived almost intact together with its magnificent mosaics, though these date from the seventh century. Again, and even more compellingly than in Santa Sabina, the apse where the altar stands is the spatial focus of the interior. Only this apse and the triumphal arch were given mosaic decoration which in other churches tended to spread to the nave as well, thus diverting attention from the single centre of attraction in the apse. As the architectural conception of the basilica has a deep symbolic meaning so has the imagery of its ornament. The subjects portrayed are not intended as naturalistic representations but as approaches to the Christian mystery of salvation from this world and entry into the Kingdom of God. The mosaic in the apse of Sant' Apollinare is concerned with Christ whose life on earth brought salvation to men. What is portrayed is the Transfiguration in which, however, the figure of Christ is replaced by the Cross in heaven with a medallion portrait of the Saviour at its centre. Vertically above appears the hand of God ready to receive the Son. Underneath, on earth, stands the patron saint of the church, St Apollinaris, in an attitude of prayer – an impressive figure clad in toga. White lambs approach from either side – the faithful seeking salvation. At the summit of the triumphal arch – a bust of Christ flanked by the symbols of the four Evangelists against a background of cloud which signifies

Rome

The Roman, it has been said, came into history with a sword in one hand and a spade in the other. Our civilisation is still Hellenistic in that its ideals of law, freedom and conduct were born in Greece. It was the Roman, however, who organised Europe and made possible, in the end, both the mediaeval and the modern worlds. If to Greece we owe art, drama, poetry, mathematics, sport and hygiene, to Rome we owe roads, bridges, water

Heaven and is sharply separated from the Earth where again lambs appear, moving towards Christ. At the sides under the springing of the arch the Archangels Michael and Gabriel stand guard; underneath them are portraits of Saints Peter and Paul. The latter link the symbolic scenes with the medalliom portraits of the bishops of Ravenna above the arcades of the nave. Series of such imagines clipeatae *are frequent in early Christian churches. They invariably begin with the Apostles or their immediate disciples and thus serve to illustrate the doctrine of Apostolic Succession. When a new bishop took possession of his church one of his first tasks was to have his portrait added to the 'gallery of ancestors'.*

supply, postal services, garrisons, town-planning, codification of law, a civil service and engineering. We also owe to Rome the imperial idea – the idea that many peoples in many lands and of many races, should live under one rule. This empire embraced the Mediterranean shore; it extended from Jerusalem to Scotland. Out of it, ultimately, were carved both the Eastern and the Western Christian churches and Islam.

We shall never know how or why that particular Latin tribe

Plate 19
ROME
Santa Sabina

Plate 20
RAVENNA
San Apollinare In Classe

Plate 21
RAVENNA
The Mausoleum of Galla
Placidia

It seems strange, at first sight, that Early Christian artists should have refrained from enriching their interiors by architectural motifs, as their pagan predecessors had done, while covering every available surface with two-dimensional, figured decoration. And even less understandable is the ousting, complete by the fifth century, of the well-established technique of wall painting by the much more complicated one of mosaic.

Yet neither of these two phenomena is accidental or inexplicable. They are the direct outcome of the preoccupation of Early Christian art with the central mysteries of the faith. Architecturally, the experience of balanced masses and structural harmonies is replaced by that of organised space – a first, abstract approach to a higher reality. This reality is then made explicit and present in the medium of mosaic whose texture – pieces of glass, paste and fragments of marble glistening with colour – has far more power to fascinate than painting. The believer thus finds himself transported into the world in which the scenes portrayed take place, the heavenly world of saints and angels.

Moreover, mosaic does not merely cover the surface of masonry but transforms its material nature. This gives full meaning to the Christian innovation of using mosaic on the walls instead of, as formerly, on the floor alone; the walls, while continuing to delimit the interior, now give direct and, as it were, bodily access to what is portrayed on them.

conquered first all Italy, then the known world. Nor is this the place to tell the story of how, out of that city on the Tiber, there emerged first the Kings of Rome, then the Republic, then the Empire; nor the story of how that Empire did not so much vanish from the earth – for in many ways it is with us still – as become transmuted beyond recognition, transmuted first into feudal Christendom, then into the sovereign states of the modern world. What matters to us is rather the story of how the Romans

This magical quality of mosaic is exemplified with greater intensity than elsewhere in the Mausoleum built in Ravenna about AD 425 for Galla Placidia, sister of the West Roman Emperor Honorius. While the marble veneer of the lower part of the wall around her sarcophagus offers a solid and tangible surface, the magnificent, toga clad figures of the Apostles in the lunettes under the crossing seem to live in a supernatural world communicating with the starry heavens in the vault. Similarly St Lawrence, fellow-countryman and patron of the deceased, emerges in the lunette at the end from an imaginary background and moves towards the gridiron with tongues of flame under it to suffer his martyr's death. The glistening surfaces give the whole interior an atmosphere of solemnity and awe, the full effect of which is better felt when light is not, as in our illustration, harshly projected from a flash-bulb but seeps through the thin sheets of marble filling the small windows.

took the ideal architectural forms of the Greek, made of them a complete architectural vocabulary, and adapted that vocabulary to an architecture which had to serve a more complex society than any the Greek could ever have imagined.

The decline of Greece was slow, but after the Periclean Age it is evident, at least by the third century BC. The architecture both of Greece itself and of her colonies in Asia Minor becomes coarser and more lavish; it loses purity and restraint. Sculpture

Plate 22
CONSTANTINOPLE
SS Sergius and Bacchus

This small church, built shortly after AD 527, shared the common fate of Christian religious edifices in Constantinople after the Turkish conquest (1453) – it was converted into a mosque. The principal victim of the change was the fresco and mosaic decoration of the interior, either whitewashed or taken down by the iconoclastic Moslems, who thus deprived the building of much of its beauty. What remained was the spatial effect characteristic of the type of church that established itself in the East in the fifth and sixth centuries. It differs radically from the Constantinian basilica with its single and imperious appeal to move forward with eye, mind and body along the nave towards the altar in the apse; in SS Sergius and Bacchus there is no such directing force. True, the church has an apsidal choir which is even emphasised by a rectangular space in front of it (see plate 23). But the choir's power of attraction is limited. The interior of which it is an easterly projection is not designed to lead to and culminate in it, but to be a self-contained whole. A spacious octagon, enclosed in an annular aisle and gallery, it revolves, directionless, under a dome round an invisible vertical axis. The entrance side is not emphasised in any way – another indication of how secondary is the longitudinal movement to the apsidal choir. The mood induced is one of concentration and stillness. These is nothing oppressive about the octagon because, generously lit from above through windows in the cupola, it offers on its sides

becomes merely pretty – although facile – or indulges in excess of violence, movement and emotion beyond the proper limits of the medium. This, as always, reflects a corresponding decadence in life itself. Plato foresaw both the decline and the decadence. He foresaw that the Greek, absorbed in the arts and luxuries of an over-ripe culture, would be unfit to defend and uphold Hellas in a world dominated more and more by Rome.

The Romans gave to history at any rate one major art form,

an alternation of semicircular and rectangular niches, conceived as open colonnades which allow the eye to penetrate into the penumbra of the circular aisle where it divines rather than discerns the enclosing walls. This, as it were, praetersensual apprehension of a spatial boundary is calculated to produce the decisive experience, that of being encompassed in an otherworldly reality – an experience that must have been far more compelling when figures of saints appeared against a gold ground and the starry heaven stretched across the cupola. In this immediacy of the divine one can well imagine the believer at first motionless then sinking to his knees in a mystical abandonment to the might of God.

one major concept – the capital city. Neither Thebes, nor Nineveh, nor Athens had been capital cities in the modern sense, as was Rome. By the time of Julius Caesar a vast empire was already being administered from the banks of the Tiber, with all that that meant in the way of official buildings and official magnificence. The Roman was very conscious of the significance of a capital as something that must impress the world, must uphold imperial dignity and must be planned therefore in the grand

Plate 21
RAVENNA
The Mausoleum of Galla
Placidia

Plate 22
CONSTANTINOPLE
SS. Sergius and Bacchus

Plate 23
RAVENNA
San Vitalc

San Vitale in Ravenna bears a striking resemblance to SS Sergius and Bacchus in Constantinople (plate 22). It consists of a similar spacious octagon communicating with a surrounding aisle and gallery through open colonnade niches – here uniformly semicircular in plan – and having on its east side the longitudinal choir illustrated here which cuts into the aisle at right angles and terminates in an apse pierced with large windows. There is no need, however, to assume that the two churches are the work of the same architect, even if it is true that they are almost contemporary. The mutual resemblance is to be accounted for in terms of what was to remain, at least until the end of the Middle Ages, a cardinal principle in art: imitation of recognised models, but not a slavish imitation, and if possible improving on the model. It is an open question whether our two churches are directly related or derive from a third building.

San Vitale is evidently the work of artists from Constantinople. Many elements point to a Byzantine derivation, in particular the trapezoid or undulating basket capitals with their carpet-like patterns of fretwork (compare plate 22) and sturdy impost blocks, and the splendidly preserved mosaics with their imperial theme and style. All this would call for no comment if the church could be safely dated after AD 540, the year in which, following Belisarius's victorious campaign, Ravenna passed from Ostrogothic to Byzantine rule and became the seat of an exarch. It has, however, been suggested

manner. The Roman was often vulgar, never mean.

With the arrival in history of the capital city therefore there came also town-planning in the grand manner. In town-planning each of the more important emperors left his impress upon the City for a period of over three centuries. Trajan was one of the great town-planners of history.

Also with the arrival of the capital city a far greater number of types of building is needed. The Greeks had, in Athens, built

that the edifice was begun in the lifetime of Theodoric the Great (died AD 526) and was intended as his palace church. This theory is not contradicted by the Eastern derivation of the architectural type. Theodoric had spent several years at the court of the East Roman Emperor before descending on Italy with an imperial commission to suppress the misgovernment of Odoacar and his Germans. He established a powerful Ostrogothic kingdom but continued to recognise the sovereignty of the Emperor, and may well have called upon Byzantine architects to adorn his capital, Ravenna. Be this as it may, the mosaics in the choir are certainly later. On the side walls of the apse appear Justinian (see plate) and his Empress, Theodora, each in solemn procession with court and church dignitaries. Next to the Emperor is Bishop Maximian, the only figure to be named in an accompanying inscription, who distinguished himself in restoring orthodoxy after the period of Arianism introduced by the Goths. The mosaics thus attest both a political and a religious triumph.

a simple, almost a vernacular town. They had reserved their architectural powers and their arts for the temples upon the Acropolis. Now in Imperial Rome it was not the temples above the city that mattered, it was the city itself – the capital city with all its multiplicity of buildings: temples, houses, theatres, markets, amphitheatres, halls, baths, libraries, avenues, triumphal arches and columns – not to mention the great fora or squares in which so many of the buildings were set. Of course the temple

98

Plate 24
CONSTANTINOPLE
Hagia Sophia

In AD 532 the principal church of Constantinople was destroyed by fire. Justinian immediately ordered a new edifice to be erected. It was to surpass everything known in size, nobility of conception and beauty of ornament and was to be completed in the shortest possible time. The architects, Anthemius of Tralles and Isidore of Miletus, were given unlimited means and, it is reported, 10,000 workmen were placed at their disposal. Hundreds of marble column shafts were hurriedly brought from ancient temples in Rome, Athens, Ephesus and even the distant Baalbek in Syria, and, in an effort quite unheard of for the time, the impossible was achieved: less than six years after work on it had begun the church stood complete to the last detail of ornament – one of the most daring and most mature architectural creations of all times, and the marvel of subsequent centuries.

The dedication was celebrated on 27 December AD 537. Justinian entering the church hastened to the pulpit and, extending his arms to heaven, exclaimed: 'Glory to God, Who has deemed me worthy of fulfilling such a work. O Solomon, I have surpassed thee!' One can well understand the imperial patron's outburst of pride. The structural excellence, the profusion of ornament in marble and mosaic, the spatial sweep of the interior to be experienced but not described – nothing like it had been seen before. And, notwithstanding subsequent alterations, the zeal of the Iconoclasts, the plunderings of the

was still important, but instead of being isolated and sacred it had now come down into the street and – like a Wren church in seventeenth century London – took its place as one building among many (*plate 10*).

This new architecture – cosmopolitan and metropolitan – demanded forms of structure far beyond anything the Greek could have mastered. Architecture, almost by definition, is the enclosure of space. And now, for Roman purposes, space had to be enclosed

Crusaders and the conversion into a mosque, the impression today is still overwhelming.

Comparison with SS Sergius and Bacchus shows interesting similarities and differences. The central portion of the interior is enclosed by aisle and gallery but on two sides only, thus approximating to a basilican nave. Yet this does not give it a longitudinal movement because it is designed as a square whose sides are spanned each by one gigantic arch resting on massive, tower-like piers at the angles and carrying a vast dome. The dome is abutted on the east and west by lower half-domes which in turn are backed by three smaller cupolae disposed in a semicircle – a gradation to be found also in SS Sergius and Bacchus. Its centrality thus emphasised, the main dome fulfils its task in a spectacular manner. It does not rise from its support but seems to float weightlessly in mid-air above a halo of light from the windows in the drum. Procopius describes it in his Buildings *as seeming 'not to rest upon solid masonry but to cover the space as though suspended by a golden chain from heaven'. To the faithful it must have appeared as heaven itself when they could see at its centre instead of a shield with Arabic characters, the image of Christ enthroned, his power radiating along the narrow bands of the vault ribs.*

on a very large scale. This could mean only one thing – engineering. Thus does the Roman come into the story of European architecture, first, as town-planner, second as an engineer, thirdly as an artist.

The Greeks, it is true, had placed their temples on the Acropolis very carefully indeed, grouping them so as to form a balanced but not symmetrical composition. It has already been said that the view of the temples from the town was vital. These were

Plate 23
RAVENNA
San Vitale

Plate 24
CONSTANTINOPLE
Hagia Sophia

Plate 25
GRAČANICA
Monastery Church

The flowering of church architecture under Justinian was of short duration. Standards began to decline rapidly and a mechanical repetitiveness set in. Wherever the Greek Orthodox Church (finally separated from Rome after the Schism of 1054) established itself – in the Balkans, on the coasts of the Black Sea, and in Russia – the type of building elaborated from earlier models in the central Byzantine lands in the ninth and tenth centuries maintained itself for centuries on end with, at best, local variations.

A good example of this persistence is the church of the Serbian monastery of Gračanica. It was built in 1321 by King Milutin, a notable patron of the arts, on Kossovo Polje, subsequently famous as the scene of two heavy battles against the Turks. The building is a scrupulous reproduction of the domed Greek Cross type as it occurred, for instance, in the Church of the Holy Apostles in Salonica. A narthex leads into the body of the church which is square in plan and intersected by two axial naves. The main dome, carried on an octagonal, fenestrated drum, rises centrally above the point of intersection while smaller and lower cupolae cover the four corners contrasting with the central dome and emphasising its dominant position.

There are also other traditional features: the loophole windows, the slender colonnettes at the angles of the drums, the arched hoods of the drum windows, the dentilled mouldings of the eaves. Even the

visual arrangements and do indeed add up to an important contribution of sorts to the art of town-planning. But a town – as we know it and as the Romans knew it – is a series of spaces – streets, squares, courts, gardens etc. – opening one out of another and giving access to building. Town-planning is the conscious arrangement of these. Such a town may be a work of art but, unlike a picture or even a single building, it is not a work of art in front of which one can stand in order to admire. It is, rather,

masonry shows an old trait in the intercalation between the white-gray ashlars of single or double courses of brick, and the ornamental use of brick and thick layers of mortar in some of the blind recesses.

a work of art through which one must progress in order to enjoy a series of contrasting moods or sensations. At the end these sensations add up to a single total sensation – grandeur, quietude, glamour or what you will. It was in this sense that the Roman understood town-planning. Because the impression he wished to make was one of grandeur, his method of planning is spoken of as being in 'the grand manner'. It is a way of planning that is magnificent, self-conscious, extravagant, ostentatious.... possibly

The main Russian principalities Kiev, Novgorod, Vladimir-Suzdal were christianised from Byzantium about the year 1000. They adopted the Byzantine style in church architecture, and, with it, though only gradually, stone as an alternative to wood in building. Though the new technique was spread by a variety of foreigners – Greeks in Kiev, Germans in Novgorod and Pskov, Lombards and Caucasians in Vladimir – Byzantine models prevailed throughout, as rigid and unchangeable as the Greek Orthodox liturgy.

The small Cathedral of St Demetrius in Vladimir (1193–1197) is a characteristic example. Like other early Russian churches it follows the simplest Greek cross type with only one, central dome on a drum. Square in plan, it has three semicircular apses on the east side while the remaining sides are flat and each have a portal so that there is no emphasised front. This formula reflects the spatial articulation of the interior which, in spite of the liturgical accent on the East end, is dominated by the central dome.

The building, however, is not merely a copy of Byzantine models. It has certain features that mark it as unmistakeably Russian. The eaves, for instance, do not run in a straight line but follow the curves of the blind arcade. Also indigenous are the reliefs on the upper storey and the window shafts of the drum. They portray Christian themes but stylize them into decorative patterns which recall Russian folk-art with its Scythian heritage, particularly textile

only practicable under a dictator. It crops up again and again in history – Baroque Vienna, Napoleonic Paris, New Delhi and so on. But it was something that Rome gave to the world.

The essence of the grand manner is that it is the opposite of the picturesque. Nothing is left to chance. Every building is given a setting; the more important or more symbolic buildings are given a setting of great magnificence. Magnificence is all.

Some monuments of Ancient Rome can still be seen and enjoyed

ornament. On the other hand, the origin of the arcade which forms a blind gallery above the portals is difficult to explain. There are distant echoes of Western Romanesque but Syrian and Armenian churches offer a better parallel. The architect may well have come from those parts.

as single buildings; they attain their full meaning only when we imagine them in their setting. This setting, whether in Rome itself or in the provincial cities of the Empire is not altogether easy to reconstruct. In the fragments that line the Via dei Fori Imperiali we can only sense the ghost of this magnificence; here and there, as in, say, Baalbek or Palmyra, we can see it more clearly; but everywhere the full and blatant majesty of marble and gilding and carving is gone forever.

Plate 25
GRADANICA
Monastery Church

Plate 26
VLADIMIR
The Cathedral of
Demetrius

Plate 27
MOSCOW
The Cathedral of
St Basil

Ivan the Terrible, the first Tsar, had this cathedral built as a thanksgiving after his capture of Kazan, the last stronghold of the Mongolian Tartars who had ruled Russia for two and a half centuries. It was built between 1555 and 1560 under the direction of two Russian architects, Postnik and Barma. The richness of form and colour contribute to making it the most characteristic and significant example of Russian religious architecture, universally considered as a symbol of the Russian spirit. The architects were not able to throw off the shackles of Byzantine tradition. Their only original contribution was to modify the cruciform plan by setting eight chapels within a square round the central tower. But the exterior reveals forces which stem from the depths of the Russian soul, an unparalleled capacity for religious experience and an uninhibited delight in the luxuriant interplay of varied forms and the powerful harmony of rich colour. From its chapels spring onion-shaped domes (painted in the seventeenth century) some ribbed, some having lozenged or other patterns; these produce the effect of a display of multicoloured fireworks spinning round the tall central tower. This blaze of colour is emphasised by the red and white decorations, and a note of the bizarre is introduced by the exaggeration of the architectural elements. In them can be seen the diverse influences — admittedly no longer clearly distinguishable — which go to make up the architecture of Russia, situated between Europe and Asia. The

Roman town-planning depended upon symmetry and balance and climax. Rome, with its seven hills, was not however a city which could be laid out symmetrically as a whole. Julius Caesar, Caesar Augustus, Nerva, Hadrian, Trajan each in turn took an area near to the older Forum Romanum, and there each added his own quota to his own glory. Each might give to the people of Rome public buildings; each might build a temple for his own deified self after death; each might add a forum — those marble

stepped arch-niches on the towers, for example, remind us of the stalactite formations in Islamic vaults, while the onion-shaped cupolas recall the curved forms of Persian domes. At the base of the building below the cluster of towers are western Renaissance columns, as well as painted coloured tiles which are also reminiscent of Persia and India. Mingled with all this are details – such as, for instance, the triangular gables – which seem to derive from native wooden architecture.

paved and colonnaded squares of Imperial Rome, rich in sculpture and looked down upon by a temple or, from far off, by the palaces on the Aventine. Trajan was really an example of what we would call a 'comprehensive planner' – his forum, triumphal arch *(plate 14)*, basilica, law courts, libraries and column were all linked together in a single planning complex. Symmetry, balance and the disposition of buildings around a great central axis were the essence of such planning. Everything in the Trajan

The chequered political history of medieval Spain is reflected in the diversity of its architecture which, at least until the thirteenth century, evolved no distinctively 'Spanish' type. The northern provinces, freed from Moorish domination in the eleventh century and made into Christian kingdoms, were largely influenced by Romanesque from the South of France. In the rest of the country, where the Moors maintained their gradually decaying power to the end of the fifteenth century, building went on in the Islamic style as it had developed locally and in other areas under Muslim rule, especially in North Africa. Finally, in some of the parts won back to Christianity, particularly along the frontier between the two faiths, there appeared, in the early thirteenth century, a mixed style known as Mudéjar *which both combined Romanesque structure with Moorish ornament and introduced Romanesque elements into Moorish structural types. Santa Maria la Blanca in Toledo, built in the early thirteenth century, is an instance of the mixed style. The interior shows little Romanesque influence. It can be discerned at best in individual features – the stocky piers, the form, though not the ornamentation, of the capitals, and the slim blind gallery arcading. But as a whole the edifice is unmistakeably a product of Moorish art, both structurally and in spatial layout. Did we not know that it was originally built as a synagogue – its conversion into a Christian church dates from the early 15th century – it could well serve as a prize example of the colonnaded mosque. The wide, almost square interior has no sense of organised direction. There are no accented lines to guide the eye*

plan led the eye from one vista to another, to culminate finally upon the Emperor's own statue within the temple. It may all have been an obvious and rather vulgar kind of planning, but the Romans did it for the first time; they did it on a big scale through their territories, and they did it well.

The repertoire of the Greeks had been limited almost wholly to the temple. The temple needed great artistry, structurally it was elementary. The Roman repertoire was large; it included

in its exploration of spatial relationships. It roams freely through a forest of short, stocky octagonal piers, not disturbed in any way by their arrangement in five rows. The piers carry typically Moorish horseshoe arches on which rest the upper walls. These have no windows and disappear, as they rise, into an uninviting penumbra. The baffled eye is set wandering again by the light which penetrates through the round windows in the lower external walls. Nor are any points of rest afforded by the ornament that covers the arcade walls and the spandrels. Its flat, geometrical patterns enrich but do not articulate them, and offer no elements of either spatial or structural rhythm.

This remarkable 'inarticulateness' of space, completely foreign to Christian church architecture, is as little of an accident as the readiness of Jewish patrons to have a synagogue erected in the style of a mosque. In neither Muslim nor Jewish worship is there altar service or liturgical celebration of any kind to determine the interior layout of the religious edifice, as there always has been in Christian worship. Moreover, in contrast to the church, neither the mosque nor the synagogue is intended as a house of God, a dwelling of the divine, but merely as a place where the individual believer or, on certain fixed days, the community, come to say their prayers. For this purpose the architectural form of the building matters little. If the Muslims adhered to the type of the colonnaded and the domical mosque (see plates 30, 31), they did so out of a feeling for tradition.

many kinds of public building and large halls. It included also the great amphitheatres and arenas – the Colosseum *(plate 12)* is only one among many – where banks of stone seats and large crowds have to be supported from below. That repertoire also included great bridges and the aqueducts *(plates 16 and 17)* which – in the absence of large pipes – were necessary to convey water supplies across valleys, or across the Campagna into Rome. (With its fountains and public baths the water consumption of

116

Plate 27
MOSCOW
The Cathedral of
St. Basil

Plate 28
TOLEDO
Santa Maria La Blanca

The jewel and climax of pure Moorish architecture in Spain, indeed one of the most splendid monuments of Islamic art anywhere is the Alhambra, the 'Red Castle' (El-Qal'at el-hamra), situated on a plateau above Granada. Built in the ninth century as a fortress, it was enlarged in the fourteenth and fifteenth into a palace for the family of the Nassarides, the last Moorish rulers in Spain (until 1492). The numerous halls, chambers and rooms cluster round two courts enclosed by light, airy arcades – the Court of the Myrtles and the Court of the Lions, the latter so called from the twelve black marble lions which support the alabaster bowl of a fountain in the centre of the court.

The arrangement of rooms round interior courtyards was an established practice, at least for larger houses, in the hot regions of the East and of North Africa. And, just as these turn their back on the outside world by plain, often windowless walls, and have, as it were, only an inner life, so the Alhambra presents an unadorned, grimly fortress-like exterior. The inside, on the contrary, displays an extravagant richness – a richness of a special, typically Islamic kind. It does not depend on architecture, on structural elements, but consists entirely of ornament which spreads like a carpet over every surface, winding round arches, climbing up to ceilings and vaults. The ornamental principle of this splendour of the Oriental fairy-tale is most apparent in the Court of the Lions. True, its delightful

ancient Rome was on a modern scale.)

The key to such large-scale structures in our time is reinforced concrete or the steel girder. For the Roman it was walling – brick, stone or concrete piled up by slave labour – and, above all, the arch. The invention of the arch is lost in the mists of time, but it was left to the Roman engineers to understand and exploit it, and thus bring about a revolution in the history of structure. The Egyptian, the Assyrian or the Greek had had to build his

arcadings with their delicate colonnettes often grouped in twos and threes, and their lanced arches of varying span — in a word its architectural elements — give it a painterly touch archieved nowhere else in the Alhambra. But were the surfaces, arches and column capitals to be stripped of their ornament — the lace-like relief of the arabesques on red and blue ground, the play of the mysteriously intertwined lines of Kufic (Old Arabic) characters, the honeycombs and stalactites of the pendants — the magic spell would be broken.

walls or columns so near together that a single stone could span from one to another. Not so the Roman. An arch consists of a series of small wedge-shaped stones called 'voussoirs'. These are supported on temporary wooden 'centring' until the keystone is in position. The centring is then removed and the stones of the arch support one another. Theoretically the arch can be built over almost any span; in practice an eighty foot span was common in the larger buildings of Rome *(plate 13)*.

In 1453 the Ottoman Turks conquered Constantinople (Byzantium). For over a thousand years it had been the residence of the East-Roman and later the Byzantine Emperors, and for several centuries its powerful walls had served as the Eastern bastion of Christendom against the onslaught of Islam. But what fell into the hands of Sultan Mehemmed II Fatih, the Conqueror, was a city living in the reflected splendour of its former glory. Its population, once a million, had shrunk to a mere 50,000, and its artistic impulse, once so fertile, had longe since died out.

But now all this changed: as the Turkish Istanbul, Der-es-Saadet (Seat of Bliss), capital of the powerful Ottoman Empire, the city flourished again. Mehemmed Fatih himself, replacing the decayed Church of the Apostles built under Justinian by a large mosque (Fatih Djami), initiated an unequalled building activity which was to make Istanbul the centre of Islamic architecture, and whose products entered into a noble contest with the monuments from the Christian period. Above all, the marvellous edifice of Hagia Sophia (plate 24), converted by Mehemmed into a mosque, imposed itself as the model to be imitated. Even Sinan (1490–1588), a genius and one of the most productive architects of all times, could not ignore the challenge. Three hundred and eighteen works stand to his credit, most of them in Istanbul. Among the most distinguished is the series of large mosques headed by that erected between 1550 and 1556 for Sultan Sulaiman I (1520–1566).

The arch exerts outward thrust. There is an Arab saying that 'the arch never sleeps'. It tries to push over the column or wall supporting it. This thrust must be resisted and thus does the buttress come into history with the arch. The medieval builders were to delight in the buttress, displaying it – whether as a flying buttress or not – as an external and decorative feature. The Romans put the outer wall of their buildings beyond the buttress, thus concealing the buttress inside the structure, but it is there

*Standing on a towering hill, the Sulaimanye appears like a monu-
mental mountain, dominated by needlelike minarets from which
the muezzin announces the times of prayer. Though the outside of
the powerful edifice is deliberately unadorned, all the opulence
Islamic artists were capable of being reserved for the interior, the
structure is almost painterly in its complex articulation. At the front
and back, flanked by smaller domes, are large half-domes leaning
against the central square over which rises the main dome (height:
174 feet). The articulation is similar to that of Hagia Sophia, and,
as there, the bare fabric of the central dome rests on a ring of narrow
windows with semicircular heads. This gives the interior the airy
lightness so characteristic of the central space of Justinian's edifice
(compare plate 24).*

all the same.

If we build a series of arches or rings one against the other
the structural principal of the arch is in no way invalidated, but
we have created a tunnel or barrel vault. This is the most elementary form of the vault, but for all that it is a true vault,
providing a permanent, fireproof and monumental roof of stone,
concrete or brick. We recall that the roof of the Parthenon was
only of wood.

Plate 31
ISTANBUL
The Mosque of
Sultan Ahmet I

When Mehmet Aga, prize pupil and successor of the celebrated Sinan built this mosque between 1609 and 1616, he also took Hagia Sophia and its Turkish imitations as his model. Here again the various units of space cluster round a central square, and half-domes – not on two but on all four sides – rise in tiers towards the crowning main cupola. The interior is thus a central space that develops evenly in all directions.

It is fruitless to attempt to read into this symmetrical central plan either systematic religious symbolism or liturgical purpose. For there is not in the Mosque of Sultan Ahmet any more than in any other domical mosque a spiritual centre to hold together the outlying spatial units, comparable, for instance, to the baptismal font in the centralised Christian baptisteries. It is remarkable, above all, that the articulation of space takes no account of two important features present in every Islamic house of prayer: the pulpit from which the Koran is read out (mimbar), and the prayer niche (mihrab). Both can be seen in our illustration; the prayer niche is no more than a shallow, apse-like recess in the wall with no architectural significance, in spite of its projecting frame. This is not accidental: the niche is not sacred like an altar sanctuary; its function, with which its remarkably modest appearance is not out of harmony, is merely to indicate the direction of the one and only sanctuary of Islam, the Kaaba in Mecca, towards which, as the prophet prescribes, the believer turns

The drawback of the barrel vault is that in order to resist its thrust at the point where it meets the wall, that wall has to be very thick throughout its whole length. (In a railway tunnel the point does not arise because the earth itself resists the thrust.) This necessity for a massive structure is not only a structural drawback – given slave labour it is not perhaps a very serious one – but it is also a practical drawback. It makes it very difficult to get daylight into the building. Where can one put windows?

his face when about to pray. In building the Mosque of Ahmet on a fully centralised plan, Mehmet Aga was, no doubt, guided by the wish to achieve an aesthetically satisfying effect by giving full value to the circular motif of the main dome.

The interior is decorated with wealth and magnificence, in a typically Islamic manner. Walls, arches and vaults are almost completely covered by a carpet of ornament. Stylised foliage of all kinds, geometrical flower motifs, oval and round shields spread over the surface (in bands and fillets). In selected places, for instance over the prayer niche, verses from the Koran are inscribed in Arabic characters the gold of whose bizarre convolutions glistens against a dark ground. The interior, lit by two hundred and sixty windows, is suffused with blue which has made the Mosque famous as the Blue Mosque. It comes from the glazed tiles, prodominantly blue with occasional streaks of red, which make up the surface decoration. This richness of colour must have been even more magnificent when all the windows still had their variegated glass shining out in bright accents against the circumambient blue, as it does to this day in the mihrab wall.

The Roman solution of this problem was a neat one. They ran one tunnel vault down the length of the building, another one across it – two intersecting barrel vaults, each a half cylinder.

This was the cross-vault. It had enormous advantages. The building, or each of the square bays into which it might be considered as being divided, now had a great semi-circular arch on each of its four sides, and under each arch – high above the 'springing' of the vault, or point of thrust – windows could be

The mausoleum which Theodoric the Great, King of the Ostrogoths, built for himself about AD 520 outside the gates of his capital, Ravenna, on what was then the coast of the Adriatic, is a peculiarly ambiguous creation. In its general layout this stern and heavy building is fully in the tradition of early Christian mausolea. Like these it is centralised in plan. A decagonal lower floor with deeply recessed niches carries a circular upper structure originally surrounded by an external arched gallery whose only extant trace are the cavities in the outside wall. One thinks of certain fifth century Byzantine ivories with representations of sepulchral buildings, two-storied and with a similar external articulation. What is unusual in the Ravenna monument is the separation of the two levels by a ceiling which destroys the spatial unity so constantly preserved elsewhere.

Also unusual is the material – heavy stone ashlar throughout, while all the other church buildings in Ravenna keep to the traditional thin brickwork. Not that either peculiarity – the intercalated ceiling or the wall of large square stone blocks – is due to lack of technical expertise. The accomplished skill evident in the cutting and placing of the ashlars in walls and arches is enough to suggest the contrary. Trained hands must have been at work here, probably Byzantine builders. It is obviously the terms of their commission that imposed a departure from usual practice.

inserted. These were above eye-level but flooded light down into the central area. This is called 'clerestory lighting' and, in one form or another, was to be inherited by the West for the lighting of its great cathedrals.

That is not the only advantage of the cross-vault on the square bay. The outward thrust of the vault is no longer along the line of the supporting wall. There is no supporting wall. The thrust is now taken down the 'groin' – or intersection line of the two

The circular structure is covered neither by a flat roof nor a dome but by a huge monolith. It is recorded that the King 'made search for a gigantic stone block with which to cover the building'. Weighing nearly five tons, the monolith is in position to this day, a flatly hollowed-out shell carrying curious 'handles' which must have served to hoist it from an earthen ramp. Its thrust accounts for the massive lower structure and the intercalated ceiling. But it remains puzzling why Theodoric should have adopted this scheme. Many explanations have been put forward, and perhaps it is the 'Romantic' one that is the most likely: the self-willed Ostrogothic ruler, conscious of his Germanic origins, carried with him memories of the tombs of his forefathers in the North of Europe – structures of large stone blocks roofed by vast, unhewn, flat boulders. It seems at least possible that Theodoric reverted to these models to display his lineage. The suggestion is also supported by the unusual ornament on the cornice. It consists of circles over triangles, and is executed in exactly the same way as the chip carvings on Germanic belt buckles and fastening needles from the period of the Barbarian Invasions. It is not clear whether the motif is a primitive, abstract rendering of foliage or a Germanic symbol for sun (circle) and earth (triangle). Be this as it may, we have here, for the first time in the history of European architecture, forms and representations that are not part of the heritage of Antiquity.

half-cylinders – and is thus concentrated at the four corners of the square bay. The walls can now be mere curtain walls, while the vault itself is supported by four massive piers or buttresses. The Romans often built such vaults on eighty foot square bays. The great public halls of the Thermae (or baths) were usually three bays long, thus giving a hall eighty feet wide and two hundred and forty feet long. The three bays of vaulting were supported by eight massive buttresses, and lit by eight large

Plate 32
RAVENNA
The Tomb of Theodoric

Plate 33
BORGUND
Church

Between the Barbarian Invasions and the reign of Charlemagne, that is from the fifth to the eighth century, Western Europe has not much to show by way of architectural achievement. The fall of the Roman Empire and the decay of its city culture had a destructive effect on antique art. The Germanic conquerors encountering its monuments in the West Roman provinces found them not only alien in spirit but so entirely new as to make impossible any kind of continuity.

By and large, they persisted in their practice; but what little survives from this period is in stone – crude first attempts to penetrate the secrets of the Roman skill. The archaeological evidence is thus doubly misleading since wooden structures, which have succumbed to rain, wind and fire, must have been both more numerous and more accomplished. Most of them were, no doubt, of no artistic value. But some buildings, such as the halls of magnates and princes, had sufficient architectural merit to move so widely travelled a man as Venantius Fortunatus, poet and, at the end of his life, bishop of Poitiers, to celebrate them in his verse. About AD 565 after a visit to the Rhineland, he praises the masterly fabric of timbered structures, their panelled interiors, the rich and curious carvings of their pergolas – and extols them above 'ashlar walls'.

We do not know what these structures looked like. But we can gain some idea of their character from the wooden churches in Norway known as stave churches. Roman stone architecture having never

clerestory windows – three on each side and one at each end. In addition the space (or aisles) between the buttresses were incorporated in the hall – in effect adding some forty feet to its width. (Note: The Basilica of Maxentius – *plate 13* – is a hall such as has been described. The ruins which we see in the picture, however, show only the aisles between the buttresses, and the big semi-circular arch on one side of one bay. The actual cross-vault is no longer there, but the stump at its springing point can be

reached Norway and Christianity reaching it only after the turn of the millennium, the field was free for Teutonic carpentry to flourish well into the Middle Ages. At one time there seem to have been over seven hundred stave churches in the country. Hardly twenty have survived, all from the twelfth or the thirteenth century, and sharing a structural family likeness. Their name comes from the Norwegian stavverk *which means stave work and indicates a fabric consisting of vertical masts, thick planks and cut shingles. The thirteenth century church of Borgund is perhaps the finest example of this group of monuments. A high central space with lower aisles and a small choir on the East is circumscribed by an exterior porch probably similar to those Venantius Fortunatus had seen in the Rhineland. The sections of shingle roofing set at a steep angle, to shake off the weight of snow, rise in tiers tapering like the branches of a fir tree, towards the ridge turret. They leave hardly any room for the vertical walls and thus give the whole a pyramidal appearance. It is not an accident that one is reminded of the heaven-storming giant towers which occur in German Gothic – products of kindred Teutonic tendencies in architecture. Also Teutonic are the remarkable dragon heads decorating the gables of the upper structure at Borgund. They recall the ornaments of Old Norse ships (e.g. the Oseberg ship) and spring, as these did, from the ancient belief that hostile demonic powers can be held in check by being confronted with their own images.*

clearly seen.)

An incidental but not unimportant advantage of the cross-vault was that the temporary wooden centring could now be reduced. Instead of constructing the 'reverse' of the whole vault in timber – supported moreover by scaffolding from the floor – only one bay at a time need be built, the centring being then dismantled and used again.

This all adds up to a very remarkable engineering achieve-

Plate 34
AIX-LA-CHAPELLE
Charlemagne's Palace
Chapel

Charlemagne's resolve to enter not only into the political but also, very deliberately, into the artistic legacy of Antiquity was of decisive importance for the development of West European architecture. In the preceding centuries of Germanic preponderance imitation of ancient monuments had been scant, arbitrary, coarse and primitive. No recognisable unified style had emerged. The advent of Charlemagne (AD 768–814) marks an epoch: the Emperor assigned to architecture a task and an aim which it had lacked and which were to become the fundamentals of what is described as Western architecture. Charlemagne ordered that churches – at that time almost the only field for artistic talent – should be built in stone and not in wood as had become common since the fall of the Roman Empire. It became a first precept for builders to proceed in the Roman manner, more Romano, *and to adhere as closely as possible to the Christian models of Late Antiquity. How seriously this programme was taken can best be seen in the large Palatine chapel at Aix-la-Chapelle, begun in AD 792 and intended both for ceremonial occasions and as a mausoleum for the Emperor.*

Built by Odo of Metz and dedicated in 805, the edifice is one of the few monuments from the Carolingian period to have come down to us almost unaltered.

The model for Aix-la-Chapelle seems to have been San Vitale in Ravenna. The structural similarities are striking and we know that

ment. Moreover, violently different though the architecture of Rome may be from Romanesque or Gothic, it does – in the vault, clerestory, aisle and buttress – contain the germ of all the great cathedrals and monastic churches for more than a thousand years thereafter.

In thus using the arch over a square the Roman created the vault. He also used the arch over a circle and thus created the dome. The dome gives us similar problems to the vault but in a

columns and capitals were brought from Ravenna for use in the new building. Moreover, San Vitale commended itself for ideological reasons: it was the imperial church in Europe, associated with Justinian, and itself similar to the Chrysotriklinos of the imperial palace in Constantinople, a fact of which Charlemagne may well have been aware. Ravenna represented for Charlemagne the Roman tradition in its living continuity, transmitted by Byzantium, but which he proceeded to reclaim for the West.

However, Aix-la-Chapelle is not a mirror image of its model. It takes over from San Vitale the scheme of a central, domed, octagonal space with an annular aisle and gallery; but there is no opening into an eastern axial choir, nor are there semi-circular recessions on the other sides of the octagon (compare plate 23). Spatial relationships thus remain unblurred: the octagon is a self-contained unit, clearly marked off from aisle and gallery. The remarkable doubling of columns in the gallery does not indicate a third storey; it was necessary because of the half-tunnel vaults placed obliquely above the gallery to carry the thrust of the high vault – a stroke of genius and an anticipation of the Gothic system of flying buttresses. In comparison with San Vitale, Aix-la-Chapelle seems heavier, more earnest, and more solemn. The powerful corner piers, the sturdy arches and mouldings speak a harsh language giving the edifice an unmistakeably Carolingian stamp.

more intractable form. The dome, like the tunnel vault, exerts thrust around its rim, tending always to burst outwards, and thus, like the tunnel vault, needs a thick supporting wall. The Romans, as we have seen, solved this in the case of the vault. They did not do so in the case of the dome. It was not fully solved until the architects of Byzantium *(plate 24)* discovered how to put a circular dome over a square plan.

The largest Roman dome, for all that, is a magnificent structure,

Plate 33
BORGUND
Church

Plate 34
AIX-LA-CHAPELLE
Charlemagne's Palace
Chapel

Plate 35
LORSCH
Royal Hall

This small, two-storeyed building is perhaps, together with Aix-la-Chapelle, the finest and best-preserved example of Carolingian architecture. It recalls an antique triumphal arch because of its groundfloor scheme of three portal-like passages framed by half-columns, and it was interpreted for a long time as a gatehouse. Its position and the arrangement of the higher floor as one unit like a hall, which is accessible by semi-circular stair turrets attached at either end, did not contradict this interpretation. But excavations have shown that it stood completely isolated in the forecourt of the abbey church of Lorsch – a large basilican structure dedicated in AD 774 of which only ruins remain – and cannot, therefore, have been a gateway. Its real purpose was to serve for imperial visits: here the emperor was ceremonially received and here he presided, perhaps enthroned in the middle archway, on solemn occasions of a non-religious character, dispensing justice and giving audiences.

The building probably dates from the reign of Louis the Pious (AD 814–840). The trend towards the imitation of Antiquity initiated by Charlemagne, though weakened, has not spent itself. In Lorsch it can be seen in the system of piers and arches set off by engaged half-columns with ornate composite capitals remarkably close to Roman models, and the series of fluted pilasters on the walls of the upper floor. But the way these elements are used is definitely

perhaps all the more magnificent because it had to be structurally so direct and so simple – an igloo taken to the nth degree. The Pantheon *(plate 11)*, or temple of all the gods, is a hundred and forty-two feet in diameter. It is circular and its dome (concrete and brick) is a half-circle. The outward thrust of the dome is met by the simplest means, by walls fifteen feet thick. There cannot, as with the cross-vault, be clerestory windows high up. So, once again, the Roman solves the problem with almost brutal directness.

not antique and shows the limitations of transplanting an artistic style from one historical context into another. Thus what is entirely lacking is the feeling for the structural cohesion of component parts, so highly developed in Antiquity. For instance, the entablature which in a Roman monument would have weighed down on the half-columns and encountered their resistance has become a narrow, flat band of ornament with a pattern of palmettes crudely executed as though by chip-carving. The pilasters of the upper floor have no structural function and are, again, purely ornamental, as are the curious triangular gables placed on top of them, a motif deriving perhaps from timber work. Finally what is completely alien to ancient practice is the ornamental treatment of wall surfaces. They are overlaid by alternately red and white tiles which mask the stone. Whether this delightful atectonic pattern has Islamic antecedents, as has been supposed, or is a formalised adaptation of the Roman brick technique known as opus reticulatum, *is of secondary importance. What matters is that the wall is treated here, as already in some Merovingian buildings (seventh and eighth century) primarily not in terms of its structural function but, in a typically Germanic manner, as a carrier of ornament.*

There is only one window in the Pantheon. This is the twenty foot diameter circular 'eye' at the dome's apex. It reduces the weight of the dome – thereby reducing thrust at the base – and at the same time lights the building dramatically.

If, in the vault, buttress and clerestory, the Roman engineer provided the structural basis for the architecture of the Western Church (Romanesque and Gothic), in showing the latent possibilities of the dome he also provided an inspiration for the Eastern

Plate 36
OBERZELL,
REICHENAU
St Georg

This small church was built about AD 890 for the monks of Oberzell on Reichenau, a small island on the Lake of Constance. It belongs to the few architectural undertakings between the middle of the ninth and the middle of the tenth century, a dark period both politically and artistically which set in after the partition of the Frankish Empire among the grandsons of Charlemagne (AD 843), and was characterised in architecture by a lapse into the coarse and the primitive.

In its layout the church remains traditionally Carolingian. Its three-aisled, flat-roofed basilican type is Early Christian as revived by Charlemagne. But, together with some of its Carolingian predecessors, it departs in one important respect from the Roman model. There is a choir not only at the East but also at the West end of the nave. The double choir is a Carolingian invention occasioned by the growing custom of dedicating churches not to one but to several saints, or else, as here in Oberzell, of devoting one choir to the cult of the patron saint and the other to that of the Saviour. Also Carolingian is the spacious hall crypt found here, as elsewhere, under the east choir whose level is thereby raised. In structure, on the other hand, the edifice bears clear marks of its own later period. The imitation of Antiquity has lost its edge, creative invention has exhausted itself, and the skills inherited from the Carolingian period are here practised on a reduced scale with a somewhat crude, rustic

or Byzantine Church. Christendom, at least in the realm of structure, owed much to Paganism.

So much for the Roman as town-planner and engineer. The story of the Roman as artist is a rather different one. Rome inherited the culture of Greece. The Roman Empire was part of an Hellenic civilisation, shot through and through with Greek ideas – drama, philosophy, science, art. In architecture the Roman took over the vocabulary of Greece – the two temple styles or

homeliness. The small size of the church may simply have corre-
sponded to the limited needs of the monastic community. But the walls
built with undressed quarry stone strike one as a relapse into pre-
Carolingian primitivism innocent of the higher skill which had been
applied at Aix-la-Chapelle (plate 34) and, partly, as late as Lorsch
(plate 35). And how awkward the attempt to give the short, stocky
columns an antique entasis! The capitals have become smooth, bell-
shaped blocks, the relief of carved ornament being replaced by flat
painted foliage. There is not a hint of structural articulation in the
walls and arches. They have the smoothness of wooden boards cut
out with a saw and put together.

The outstanding artistic interest of the church is in its wonderful
wall paintings executed at the end of the tenth century. In a rare
state of preservation, and perhaps the finest cycle of frescoes known to
us from the early Middle Ages, they completely cover the walls of
the nave with figures of saints and miracle scenes from the Life of
Christ. It is significant that there is little correspondence between
painted decoration and underlying structure. The fret bands bound-
ing the frescoes above and below look like substitutes for carved
mouldings; but this intention is contradicted by the illusionist effects
of spatial depth in their rendering. The strips of perpendicular
ornament separating the individual paintings are not in any way
accorded with the axes of the windows above or of the arcades
below. The painted surface leads an entirely autonomous existence.

'orders' from the Acropolis, Doric and Ionic, as well as the third
and more ornamental one, the Corinthian *(plate 8)*. Significantly
it was the Corinthian order that the Roman preferred. He used
these Greek orders not logically and with restraint, as the Greeks
had done, but as an ornamental system for tricking out his basically functional structure. For example, we see how on the Colosseum
(plate 12), the arches – part of a complex system for supporting
the seats round the arena – are framed in by the orders in the

Plate 35
LORSCH
Royal Hall

Plate 36
OBERZELL,
REICHENAU
St. Georg

Plate 37
HILDESHEIM
St Michael

The proud, castle-like structure of St Michael (begun before 1010, completed 1033) marks the advent of German Romanesque. Its size and appearance testify both to the political restoration, under the Ottonians, of the Holy Roman Empire of the German nation, and to the revival of artistic impetus about the turn of the millennium. In many respects St Michael harks back to Carolingian models, for instance in the doubling of choir and transept and in making the exterior monumental by adding towers. But it is at once evident that the general conception is entirely new. There are no more echoes of Antiquity, whether direct or mediated through the Carolingian tradition, the latter being drawn upon only in its original aspect. The new style lacks refinement and elegance but with all its austerity it speaks a language of incomparable clarity. Dominated by the sober, unornamented uniformity of the fabric, the various parts of the building – distinct, self-contained solids – make up a powerful and imposing whole. With the impression of solemnity goes one of balance, the result of the symmetrical grouping of structural elements but also of an interaction between horizontal and vertical relationships: the groups of towers, weighing down rather than rising, hold in check the development of the nave and transepts. All movement is arrested, it comes back on itself and confers on the whole a stability of presence until then unknown in church architecture.

form of ornament attached to the wall – Doric on the ground-floor, Ionic above and Corinthian above that. These have no structural meaning and have in effect been degraded to a mere 'style' or convention *(plate 14)*. In such purely functional and engineering works as the Pont du Gard – the great aqueduct near Nîmes *(plate 17)* – where no civic magnificence was wanted – the conventional orders are omitted. Moreover, the projecting corbels which supported the scaffolding and centring are left as they were the day the building was finished .... yet the Pont du Gard is more impressive, more honest, than all the temples in Rome.

In his actual decoration of his structure the Roman, again, may be contrasted with the Greek. With slave labour he could pile up the thick walls and the buttresses. It was a system of mass. The Greek had carved the actual stones of the structure – delicate flutings of columns, the Parthenon frieze and so on – but the

Plate 38
ALPIRSBACH
Abbey Church

The movement for monastic reform begun at Cluny reached Germany in the eleventh century. Hirsau in the Black Forest became its principal bridgehead from which it soon spread to numerous other monasteries. The purpose of the movement was not only to win the monks back to ascetic otherworldliness, the pursuit of which had slackened considerably, but also to elaborate a style of monastic architecture in keeping with an austere way of life. The Roman basilica, the archetype of the Christian church, was again taken as a model, while at the same time the recent tendency to excessive enrichment, whether architectural or purely decorative, was proscribed. Churches, particularly interiors, were to be deliberately sober in appearance, renouncing elaborate decoration, a reflection and a reminder of what was expected of the monks themselves.

The twelfth century monastic church of Alpirsbach, directly descended from Hirsau is a good example of the Cluniac trend in architecture. Its three-aisled, flat-roofed interior (see plate) has an austere severity. The powerful columns with their typically Romanesque bases and cushion capitals carry round arches neatly cut out of the wall. The walls above with their undifferentiated surfaces seem to hem in the space between them by their sheer verticality, a feature to be observed also elsewhere in this period. A simple moulding, no more than one unornamented course extending at right angles the sill of

Roman, while also carving over-lavishly his marble buildings, could hardly do the same with his vast piles of brick and concrete. So he evolved a decorative system which gave him all the ornament and colour he wanted. It involved *covering* the structure, as opposed to carving it – plaster, mosaic, paint or thin sheets of marble. In the Basilica of Maxentius *(plate 13)* we can see the holes in the brickwork where the bronze clamps held the marble sheets to the wall. To-day as we gaze upon such vast remains

155

the gallery in the entrance wall, runs continuously above the arcades moderating the effect of steepness and assisting the movement of the nave towards the choir.

we are impressed by structural daring and by sheer size – but this is only the carcass which the Roman once covered with an excess of ornament and colour in tune with his character.

Only now and again did the Roman – in the guise of the wealthy connoisseur – ask for refinement and sensitivity in his art. Then, almost always, he employed a Greek. Rome and the Roman world were full of Greek artists. They were in demand and the more discerning patrician knew how to use them.

Plate 37
HILDESHEIM
St. Michael

Plate 38
ALPIRSBACH
Abbey Church

Plate 39
MARMOUTIER
Abbey Church

The task of giving the church façade an appearance commensurate with its importance spurred Romanesque builders to ever new, imposing achievements. Here was the opportunity to bring out the potentialities of the exterior by scupltural means and to enhance its dignity by erecting towers. Contrary to the universality of Gothic which was yet to come, the Romanesque façade varies from country to country, indeed from region to region. While Italy and Southern France place their portals in the midst of richly ornamented, towerless show-pieces (plate 53), and Northern France elaborates the twin-tower façade so important for the future, Germany, whose most important churches are of the double choir type without a façade, continues largely to cultivate the Carolingian westwork. The finest example is the west end of Marmoutier in Alsace (twelfth century). It follows very closely its ninth and tenth century forerunners and is, like these, an almost independent structure crowned by towers whose galleries enclose a narthex-like interior. The grouping of the towers also follows the old models: the sturdy recessed block of the belfry in the middle is flanked by turrets flush with the façade. In other respects, however, there is a fine display of the Romanesque sense of form. The delightful interplay of shape and height in the three towers is counterpointed by the three flat gables at the top of the façade. The middle gable, doutbless not accidentally, is lower than the two side ones – a reversal of what obtains between the towers.

Early Christian

Rome, in the latter days of the Empire, was a cosmopolitan city. It was a melting pot for all the mixed races of the known world. It was also a melting pot for all the strange, dark cults, superstitions and religions of that world. Officially Rome had taken over the Olympic deities of Greece – giving them new Latin names – but the materialistic Roman was sceptical and tolerant in religious matters. Local gods were worshipped among the

The result is an ensemble whose rhythmical cohesion is of a very individual kind. The lively, pronouncedly three-dimensional effect of the towers comes all the more into its own as the façade, in spite of a fine articulation with pilaster strips, round arch friezes and horizontal mouldings, remains shallow. This in turn benefits the entrance. It is at the back of a vaulted vestibule which is opened by an arcade of three arches and, like a dark cavern, immediately attracts the eye.

conquered peoples throughout the Empire, while in Rome itself Mithras, Isis, Cybele and Christ were all worshipped side by side with Venus and Jupiter.

Rome also had a vast proletariat – slaves, beggars, mercenaries, under-dogs of all kinds – housed in ramshackle tenements, people without hope. When, therefore, the first apostles brought the teachings of Jesus to Rome they were sowing their seed on fertile soil. Official Rome regarded them as just one more harmless

Plate 40
COLOGNE
Church of the Holy
Apostles

Just as European Romanesque façades vary from region to region, so do east ends (compare plate 46). One of the most curious is the so-called trefoil-plan as it appears – amongst other churches in the Rhineland, particularly Cologne – in the church of the Holy Apostles (c. 1200). The short arms of choir and transept are in the form of semicircular apses, so that the eastern part of the church becomes a kind of centralised structure with equal members arranged at three sides of the central space of the crossing.

The exterior of the trefoil of the Holy Apostles is among the most mature achievements of German High Romanesque. Its hallmark is balance and calm. The lower part of the structure rests on the ground broadly and solidly. The effect is further emphasized by the compactness of the octagonal crossing tower but counteracted by the slender flanking towers. These are carried high enough to relieve the oppressive weight of the body of the building and strike a balance between the horizontal and the vertical.

The same principle operates in the articulation of the wall surface: against the horizontal mouldings and arcadings stand the vertical pilaster strips and colonnettes. But particularly satisfying is the way in which the wall surface opens up and submits to differentiation in the three stages of its ascent. The pilaster strips of the lowest zone, of almost linear flatness, are succeeded higher up by the more plastic columns of a blind arcade, while under the eaves the wall gives way

sect. Only later, when Jesus sometimes seemed to rival Caesar, did persecution begin. To the Roman proletariat Christian teaching made a tremendous appeal. The 'gods' had become the gods only of the ruling class; whereas Christianity implied a complete transposition of values. The Roman worship of power and wealth, of gluttony, sadism and sensuality were now replaced by the Sermon on the Mount.

Three centuries were to pass before Christianity became the

completely to the closely spaced openings of a gallery. The delight-
ful play of light and shadow thus increases with height, contributing
to the final complex balance in which the progressive articulation of
the three zones, as they rise above one another, is accompanied at
each stage by a decrease in mass and height. Unfortunately the
damage which the Church of the Apostles suffered in the last war has
affected much of its east end, and particularly the gallery which has
not yet been satisfactorily restored.

official religion of the dying Empire, before Constantine was
baptised and the symbols of Christ were placed on the standards
of the Legions. Those years were not wholly a time of persecution
– there were long intervening periods of toleration – nor were
those years spent wholly in the catacombs. Already this new
Christian sect was feeling its way towards an architecture of its
own, towards a form of building wherein the priest, in view of
the congregation, could celebrate the very simple rites of the

Plate 39
MARMOUTIER
Abbey Church

Plate 40
COLOGNE
Church of the Holy
Apostles

Plate 41
WORMS
Cathedral

The Cathedral of Worms, which with Speyer and Mainz forms the proud trinity of Romanesque imperial minsters in the Rhineland, and resembles them in its double choir plan, was begun after 1081 but completed only in the first half of the thirteenth century with the erection of the monumental west end (see plate). At a time when French Gothic was achieving its finest and most mature in the Cathedral of Amiens, when Gothic held undivided sway in England, when Germany too was becoming increasingly receptive to the new style, at Worms the specifically German conservative attachment to Romanesque proved stronger than the trend towards innovation. True, the Romanesque of this attractive building is long past its zenith; its declining energies are directed towards wealth of ornament rather than harmony of proportion. Two slender circular towers flank a heavy octagonal tower, all but squash it between them (the impression is intensified by the broad proportions of the west choir), carry it in their ascent and at the same time depress it by their own superior height. The polygonal choir abutting on this trio of towers is too heavy for it. Yet, though the sense of structural balance seems to have given out, the other great quality of Romanesque, the three-dimensional articulation of the wall surface is still in full vigour.

In the choir walls particularly, undifferentiated surfaces give way almost completely to a variegated pattern of blind arcadings and

Last Supper. The church, as opposed to the shrine or temple, had come into history.

But the Christians were a poor sect, and they certainly could not, in those early centuries, emulate the great marble halls of the Thermae. Nor did they want to. There were simpler forms of building in Rome and it was in private houses or small halls that the Early Christians first worshipped.

In its extreme simplicity, humility and lack of sophistication

*round windows. This engenders a rich play of light and shadow
and stimulates the feeling for volume and mass – both characteristic
of Romanesque architecture.*

the earliest buildings used as churches must have been very moving,
very impressive – not least in Rome itself, surrounded by the
monuments of Paganism.

When, in due course, churches did come to be built they were
called 'basilicas' from the Pagan type upon which they were
based. The Basilica of Trajan for example – though a large
building – was not by Roman standards a very lavish one. It
was a sort of bourse or market and general place of assembly.

Plate 42
LIMBURG on the
LAHN
Cathedral

Strikingly situated on a high throne of rock, the Cathedral of Limburg towers like an imposing citadel of God over the river and the swarming roofs of the town. Completed in 1235, it is an example of the so-called transitional style, characterised by the adoption from French Gothic of various isolated motifs, for instance the pointed arch and the buttress, into what remains fundamentally a Romanesque edifice. Limburg shows this conservative tendency clearly. There is an evident wish to follow the architectural lead given by France but the model chosen is Laon (plate 49), a remarkably old-fashioned cathedral with little in common with such pioneers of the new movement as Paris, Chartres or Reims. No doubt the close ecclesiastical links between Limburg and Laon go some way towards explaining the choice, but it is also clear that in purely architectural terms the German builders were receptive to the 'conservatism' of Laon and not to 'progressive' French Gothic. The debt to Laon is considerable: inside, the four zone division of the walls and the sexpartite rib vaults; outside, particularly the flanking of the transepts with slender corner towers. These – in Laon planned but only partially executed – together with the high crossing tower and the sturdy pair of the west front give the building a truly fortress-like appearance. What makes the impression so compelling is the unusual shortness of the nave and the resulting proximity to one another of the two tower groups which gives the whole a wonderful compactness.

It had a large central hall with columned aisles on either side; it had a clerestory above the aisles. It had not, however, a vault, only a timber roof. This type of building – since the timber roof needed comparatively slender walls and columns to support it – gave a good clear floor space, good light and economy in building. This, therefore, was the prototype of the Christian churches. What had to be added was a recess or large semicircular apse at one end where the service could be conducted. The Christian

The adoption of important Gothic features notwithstanding, the exterior is constructed in an unmistakeably Romanesque manner. The distinctness of the various parts, the additive composition of the west towers by a series of sharply outlined cubes, the manifold articulation of the walls, and, not least, the balanced distribution of the towers which arrests the flow towards the east end and brings the building to a firm rest – all this comes from the tradition of Romanesque.

never quite rid his mind of an older Pagan ritual, and so, the apse is designed both for a priesthood and an altar *(plates 19 and 20)*. The moment Christianity becomes a 'Church' it not only acquires an architecture, but it begins to organise and develop that architecture for a rubric and a ritual, and as an expression of emotions and aspirations.

These churches consisted of a simple hall with a timber roof, with columns opening out into aisles on each side and with the

Plate 41

WORMS
Cathedral

Plate 43
ST SAVIN-sur-
GARTEMPE
Church

France, politically disunited, took much longer than Germany to recover from the architectural decline of the ninth and tenth centuries. Not until the first half of the eleventh century did a revival set in, slow at first, but then, from the twelfth century onwards, developing with a sweep unparalleled in previous French history. In accordance with prevailing fashion the style adopted was Romanesque and, as in Germany, the pressing, almost exclusive task was the building of churches. However, Romanesque as practised by French masons had a character of its own which varied from region to region reflecting, so it would seem, the political divisions of the various parts of the country (see plates 44 to 49).

In the south, the predominant type is the tunnel-vaulted hall church. St Savin-sur-Gartempe, dating from about 1080, is an example. Tall, closely spaced, cylindrical pillars carry a powerful central tunnel vault decorated by the celebrated paintings known as the Bible of St Savin (early twelfth century). The edifice is one of the earliest to make use of vaulting, revived for the first time since Antiquity, not only for crypts and so on but for the main body of the church. The windowless nave is flanked by relatively wide aisles which give it light and whose somewhat lower groin vaults take the side thrust of the central tunnel-vault. The rapid succession of the pillars, the unhindered run of the arches and the continuous flow of the vault impart to the nave, in spite of its steepness, a directed

clerestory windows above. At the far end was the apse with altar and clergy seats and – if the church was a cathedral – the bishop's throne behind the altar. Sta Sabina, Rome *(plate 19)* or the little church at Torcello, outside Venice, do give one some idea of the first churches the Christians built.

Ornament was sparse but such wall paintings as there were began, even in early times, to be concentrated in certain places. The blank wall above the aisle columns and below the clerestory

movement comparable to that of the Early Christian basilica. Never-theless the interior is unmistakably Romanesque. Its atmosphere is quite individual. It is determined by the weight and sturdiness of the various parts, by the smoothness of the masonry and the thrust of the heavily resting vault. The early Romanesque predilection for solidity and mass is here clearly in evidence.

windows was usually devoted to male saints on one side of the church, to female saints on the other side – all moving towards the apse. The semi-dome over the apse, above the altar, usually showed Christ in Majesty, Christ Pantocrator, with the apostles; Christ's baptism was also sometimes incorporated in the design. This established a tradition which was to continue down the ages.

For more than a thousand years the Western Church (i.e. the village churches, monastic churches and cathedrals of Western

Plate 44
VEZELAY
La Madeleine

This sturdy abbey church, apart from the Gothic East end, is a work of the early twelfth century. A basilica with nave and aisles, but no gallery, vaulted throughout, it is a product of the so-called Burgundian school of French Romanesque, and one of the most mature, though in many respects it departs from the type. Much of what gives the other Burgundian churches of the period their unmistakable stamp is omitted in Vézelay. Thus, except in the narthex, the pointed arch is not to be seen, a neglect all the more significant as Burgundy was the first to break the monopoly of the round arch and adopt as a regular feature the pointed one, undoubtedly derived from Islamic architecture which the First Crusade (1096) had revealed to the West. Also absent is the fluted pilaster often crowned with an ornate Corinthian capital, an antique feature preserved in the numerous Roman structures of the region and used in other churches as a variant of the columnar respond.

But the most striking departure from type is in the vaulting. The normal variety for the nave in this period is the pointed tunnel vault established as part of the Burgundian church type at the turn of the century by the no longer extant but well attested third church of Cluny, the monastic centre so important for the artistic and cultural history of Western Europe. The use of the tunnel vault was no doubt dictated by the wish to give the church interior a continuous flow from portal to chancel, as in the Early Christian basilica which the

Europe), despite their vast stylistic developments – which we call Romanesque and Gothic – was really expanding and elaborating the plan form of the Early Christian basilica. Of course as the centuries passed the outward form of the architecture changed out of all recognition. To the plain basilican form there came to be applied Roman principles of vaulting, and these in turn changed, in Gothic architecture, into something more intricate and flexible than a Roman could have dreamt of. For all this,

179

Cluniac programme took for its model. Vézelay, on the contrary,
uses a groin vault which breaks up the ceiling into a series of distinct
sections, so many intervals in the movement from west to east. The
heavy transverse arches with their alternately white and grey
voussoirs, spanning the nave like bridges, and the plastically
emphasized half columns carrying them enhance this arresting effect.
And yet the overall impression is not one of an 'additive' collection
of autonomous parts. The uniformity and regular succession of the
arches and the vertical members, counterpointed by the alternating
colour rhythm, divisions notwithstanding, ensures the movement
towards the chancel.

one thing persisted in the Western Church to the end – the
basilican plan. The simple basilican hall, with columned aisles,
was the germ of the nave – that area of the church reserved for
the laity. The simple basilican apse, on the other hand, underwent a much greater transformation. It grew and blossomed
through the centuries. As the services and ritual became more
elaborate, and the number of choir and clergy increased, so the
eastern limb of the church had grafted onto it chancel, choir,

Plate 43
ST. SAVIN-sur-
GARTEMPE
Church

Plate 44
VEZELAY
Ste. Madeleine

Plate 45
ANGOULEME
St Pierre

The domed churches of Aquitaine are among the most remarkable creations of French Romanesque. Dating all from the twelfth century, they form a small, isolated group clearly marked off by its use of domed vaulting from architectural practice in the neighbouring regions. Their origin has not been established, but the influence of Byzantine architecture can be safely surmised since in it alone are comparable domed structures to be found. Moreover, one of the early and principal works of the group, St Front in Périgueux (after 1120), seems to have been inspired by San Marco in Venice (plate 54) if not by the latter's model in Constantinople, Justinian's Church of the Apostles. Like these it has a Greek cross plan and is roofed by five large domes on pendentives. However, the other Aquitanian churches are longitudinal structures with transepts, of distinct spatial units each covered and are made up by a dome.

St Pierre at Angoulême (first half of the twelfth century) has a nave consisting of three domed units. With their powerful corner piers, heavy arches and high vaults, they lead a self-contained, autonomous existence. Nowhere else is the Romanesque principle of the interior as a sum of distinct parts applied in so extreme a fashion. And few buildings of the period testify so forcefully to the Romanesque sense of volume, its bold projection into space in the

presbytery, ambulatory, chapels, Lady Chapel and so on. But always this eastern limb of the church – like its germ, the apse – was reserved for the clergy. Indeed the story of the *plan* of the church in the West – as distinct from the more complex story of structure and decoration – is really the story of the eastern limb; the nave remained in essence unchanged.

So out of the Early Christian basilica there evolved in the course of centuries our long Western plan, with the long vista

shaping of individual members, or to its preference for the austere
language of bare stone-work, as do St Pierre and the other churches
of the group. As though hewn out of a boulder, transparently clear
in its design and without any superfluous ornament, St Pierre has a
monumentality which seems to remove it outside time.

down the columned aisle and chancel to the high altar at the far end. Dividing screens and the long perspective gave mystery and drama to the whole. Every variation was ultimately played upon this theme .... but the long west to east perspective of, say, Chartres or Lincoln is there only because of the shape of the first Christian churches in Rome.

Already, however, even in Early Christian times the plan was becoming inadequate. At a very early date, for example, a railed in

186

Plate 46
TOULOUSE
St Sernin

The imposing structure of St Sernin (chancel dedicated in 1096; the whole completed in the second half of the twelfth century), with a double-aisled nave and an aisled transept, exemplifies the type, particularly favoured in Auvergne, of the church with gallery but no clerestory.

The tunnel vaulted nave is windowless as, for instance, at St Savin-sur-Gartempe (plate 43), but its arcades are not carried all the way up to the springing of the vault, the inner aisles being divided into groundfloor and gallery. The arrangement is reflected in the exterior: the south transept and the chancel, to be seen on our plate, show the two-level fenestration of the aisles which encompasses the only slightly higher nave. This harmony between interior and exterior is a fundamental characteristic of Romanesque. No less typical is the autonomy of the various structural elements, nonetheless clearly marked for being counteracted by a system of plastic decoration that makes for unity. Heinrich Wölfflin's remark that the parts of a Romanesque building could be separated from each other 'without bloodshed' is well illustrated in the exceptionally fine crossing tower and the harmonious grouping of the chancel. The tower is in five stages, marked off by sturdy cornices, so many blocks in vertical juxtaposition. As for the chancel, the high inner rotunda, the ambulatory and the radiating chapels each retain their individuality.

space for the choir had to be made jutting out into the nave – there being of course no room for it in the apse. These railings or *cancelli* gave us our word 'chancel', and clearly they imply the need for an eastern limb. Also at an early date we find secondary apses at the end of the aisles, having their own altars for saints or martyrs. One day, centuries on, the French cathedrals were to be ringed at their eastern end with a chevet of chapels. Thus do we see the start of the long story of the architecture of the Western church.

Plate 45
ANGOULEME
St. Pierre

Plate 46
TOULOUSE
St. Sernin

Plate 47
JUMIEGES
Abbey Church

This early work of the Norman school, dedicated in 1067, is a flat-roofed basilica (roofing not extant), with triforium, clerestory, a powerful crossing tower, and two-storeyed chancel. Though now in ruins it is a great art-historical interest, especially on account of a feature of its nave arcade, the alternation of circular and polygonal supports – columns and rectangular compound piers – instead of the usual homogeneous series of either the one or the other. The feature appears already in early works of German Romanesque (Gernrode, 962; St Michael, Hildesheim, c. 1020) but, whereas in these the rhythmical effect so achieved is confined to the arcade zone, the Norman builders invade the wall surface above, which in the German examples is traditionally plain and uninterrupted in its horizontal flow.

In Jumièges the piers each have a frontally attached demi-shaft which rises to roof level creating a strong counter emphasis to the horizontal division into storeys and breaking up the wall into vertical fields. Here, then, for the first time in the history of Western architecture – if the accident of survival is not misleading – the principle of the horizontal articulation of the wall surface has been discarded. The fact that this should have happened in the region of Norman settlement has given rise to various theories, especially as the articulating system has, in Jumièges, no structural justifictaion – the stout walls are quite sufficient for supporting the wooden roof

Byzantine

Two great architectural streams went out from Rome – one westwards, based on the basilica and the cross-vault, and one eastwards based on the dome. The western stream – as we shall see in Romanesque and Gothic – involved the application of vaulting to the long basilican plan with its nave, chancel and chapels. The eastern stream – the Byzantine – wrestled instead with the problem of the dome. The essence of that problem was

— and must have been devised on purely aesthetic grounds. However, it will not do to say, as has been sometimes said, that on becoming sedentary (their settlement in Northern France dates from 911) the Normans, these last Germanic migrators, sublimated their longing for distant lands and seas into a spiritual aspiration upwards, which they sought to express in the vertical emphasis of their church interiors. There may be a grain of truth in this explanation but it seems more to the point to see in the shafts of Jumièges a legacy of Germanic timber constructions, with their upright posts and consequent pronounced verticality.

to place a dome over a plan more elaborate and more flexible than the mere circle of the Roman Pantheon. The Pantheon had had a noble simplicity but was singularly inadaptable; indeed it was a functionally impossible plan for a church with a fully developed ritual. For all that the dome had obvious attractions. It was simple, grand and monumental. On a large scale it gave a very large floor area free from columns or piers. A central dome gave great unity to the entire building, however complex that building

Plate 48
CAEN
St Etienne

The nave of this edifice, a basilica with gallery and clerestory, built between 1064 and 1077, originally had flat wooden roofing. When this was replaced, about 1100, by a stone vault, the already existing shafts engaged in the nave wall were used in a way that was to be important for further structural development. The type of vault adopted was the groin vault, but with an elaboration on the ordinary system of plain cells and transverse arches as it had been applied in the aisles, and as it appears, for instance, in the roughly contemporary nave of the Cathedral of Speyer. The elaboration consisted in emphasising the groin arris by a heavy, moulded stone fillet. These fillets, serving no structural purpose, continue in the ceiling the decorative articulation of the nave wall by engaged shafts, which we have seen in Jumièges (plate 47), but in doing so they justify the shafts structurally, in that these now act as responds. The fillets are embedded in the masonry of the vault, an integral part of it. The coming decades would discover that by being disengaged and converted into a framework of rib arches they could become the essential component of a new type of vault, whose much thinner layer of masonry is filled in after the ribbing has been mounted. This transformation would be a decisive step towards Gothic which required the light rib vault to achieve its aims of attenuated fabric and vertically emphasised structure.

might be in the number of its subordinate parts.

If the vault, repeated over a series of bays, was ideally suited for roofing the long western plan, then the dome, in its turn, seems to almost require a 'centralised' plan – that is, a plan which is symmetrical about a point: square, octagon, circle or some kind of equal-armed cross. The ritual of the Byzantine Church could then move and revolve, like some tremendous ballet, in a central spacc with a great dome above.

As the story of Gothic in Western Europe is virtually the story of vault development through Spain, France, Germany and England; so we find that the story of Byzantine architecture is virtually the story of dome development through the Byzantine territories of Eastern Italy, all through Greece and what are now the Balkans, and so right up through Russia *(plates 25, 26 and 27)* to the point where the 'onion' domes of the Baltic are found over the vaulted Gothic churches of Scandinavia . . . . . thus

196

Plate 47
JUMIEGES
Abbey Church

Plate 48
CAEN
St. Etienne

Plate 49
LAON
Cathedral

Begun about 1060 and completed towards 1210, with the transept and the first three bays of the choir as the oldest surviving portions, this powerful edifice marks the transition to Gothic. Comparison with Romanesque churches, such as St Etienne in Caen (plate 48), shows that a new spirit is at work. The almost oppressive weight and bold volume of the masonry have given way to a fine-membered lightness, the gloomy solemnity of the interior has been lit up. The pointed arch, so characteristic of Gothic, has almost entirely ousted the Romanesque round one, confined here to the arcade of the narrow triforium. Above all, the upward drive, the soaring of space and structure to the distant vaults which will be the hallmark of Gothic interiors, appears, at least at first sight, to be already in operation. Yet, though these forward looking features are undoubtedly important, the architecture of the church remains basically conservative. For instance, the crossing preserves the character of a spatial focus in that it ceiled is not at the same level as the adjacent parts but rises into a light, open tower shaft. The nave and the chancel converge on this centre but do not absorb it into a continuous spatial flow as will be the case in Gothic structures. The same occurs in the transversal axis of the transepts whose relatively long arms – again a Romanesque feature – each constitute a separate unit. The conception of the whole as a sum of self-contained parts operates also in the vaulting. Sexpartite as in Caen, it consists of

completing the circle that had its starting point in Rome.

Under pressure of Goth and Vandal the Emperor Constantine, in the fourth century, had established the Eastern Empire. He gave it a great capital on the Bosphorus – a 'New Rome' that was called after him – Constantinople. There it remained for over a thousand years until sacked by the Turks in 1453 – in some ways more Roman than Rome. It was Imperial and Theocratic. The Roman genius for daring structure and engineering was now

two-bay compartments whose autonomy is emphasised above by the ribs converging towards a common centre, and at the sides by the alternation in the number of vaulting shafts. The system is at its most complete immediately west of the crossing where the alternation is carried down to the ground, every second pier being flanked by five colonnettes.

The treatment of the nave walls is also conservative. While in mature Gothic the wall is disembodied and largely replaced by glass, here its fabric is not denied as such but only plastically diversified. True, the arcades of the gallery and the triforium eliminate a large part of the surface but they seem hollowed out of it and thus respect its materiality, indeed enhance it by the sculptural effects of light and shadow. Thus the two middle storeys exist in their own right, separating the individual sections of the wall from the upward movement of the vaulting shafts. The alternation in the number of these acts as a further restraint, imparting as it does a horizontal rhythm to the wall. And the shafts are themselves checked in their ascent by their numerous rings and the projecting cornices at each level, while being deprived, as it were, of an initial momentum by the fact that the groundfloor piers do not in any way accord with them. Paramount verticality, from ground to vault, is still in the future, reserved for fully mature Gothic; here in Laon, the interior continues horizontally at rest.

applied to Christian instead of to Pagan building – but it was the same genius – while the Greek and oriental artists were more numerous even than they had been in Rome.

But by the time of Constantine the simplicity and humility of the primitive church had passed. Already the Byzantine Church was elaborately organised, with a hierarchy, wealth and Imperial patronage. Its faith was implicit. It was obsessed with the sacerdotal and the supernatural, with the sins and wickedness of this

Plate 50
PETERBOROUGH
Cathedral

The Norman Conquest created the conditions for the first really significant period in English architecture. The invaders brought with them a fully developed style, Norman Romanesque (compare plates 47 and 48), and imposed it almost under compulsion, not least as a token of their dominion. The Conquest was directly followed by a period of feverish building. The imported style was so foreign to the native English that most of the master builders had to be brought from the Continent. And yet the Anglo-Saxon tradition, though officially discarded, re-asserted itself in various ways within the new style.

The abbey church of Peterborough (choir 1118–1143, nave 1197), raised to cathedral status in 1541, is a good example of this underground survival. Nave, chancel and transept are grouped in the usual manner as autonomous units round the tower shaft of the crossing but depart from Continental models in their length and their almost Gothic loftiness. Both these features appear in the modest churches that have survived from Anglo-Saxon times, and at least one of them, the tendency to very long interiors, was to persist for centuries (compare plate 68). Another constant habit is the serial repetition of one architectural element – for instance a narrow bay framed by slender shafts is repeated to make up the nave walls of Peterborough. The same principle operates in the division

world, the bliss or agonising torments of the next. Asceticism, chastity and flagellation were the way to Paradise. An unearthly solemnity, an unearthly music; grim, gloomy and bearded saints, half-light, and glowing but cavernous churches are all part of the essence of Byzantine art. Once again – as in all great epochs – all things combine together to produce an architecture in which art and structure and religion give to us an elaborate unity.

The structural problem of the dome was in essence the same

into storeys. Groundfloor, gallery and clerestory though structurally differing from each other, are roughly equal in height. Finally – another persistent trait of English architecture – the wall is resolved into a three-storey arcade comparable to a Roman aqueduct. This together with the grid-like treatment of what little solid surface is left results in an approximation to the Gothic trellis without, however, achieving the refinement of the later creation.

as that of the vault. The vault – or at any rate the simple tunnel vault – is really a series of arches over a square or rectangular plan. Their outward thrust must be resisted by a thickening of the wall until – as we have seen – the cross-vault is evolved so as to give an arch on each of the four sides of the bay, and to concentrate all the thrust onto four piers at the four corners. The dome – as we have seen in the case of the Pantheon – needs a thick wall *all round* the circle. Only if we can discover how to

Plate 49
LAON
Cathedral

Plate 50
PETERBOROUGH
Cathedral

Plate 51
GLOUCESTER
Cathedral

Of the massive Romanesque church that the Benedictines of Gloucester built for themselves between 1089 and 1121 only the nave has preserved, more or less, its original appearance. As in Peterborough (plate 50), though in an entirely different fashion, Norman Romanesque was drawn upon and modified to give a peculiarly English result. Powerful, tower-like round piers (31 feet high, 6¹/₂ feet in diameter) carry the heavy, richly moulded arches of the ground floor. Contrary to Continental practice, partly followed in Peterborough, the piers are not in any way adapted to the mouldings of the arches; they stand out as autonomous entities, their sturdy shafts attesting the Romanesque predilection for bold effects of volume in space. Unusual also is the upward drive which raises the groundfloor arcade to almost half the height of the entire wall, its openings thus acquiring gigantic dimensions. The depressed, horizontally emphasised triforium acts as a sudden brake. The movement is taken up again by the clerestory – cut into and diminished in height by the low-set springing of the Gothic rib vault (which replaced, about 1240, the original flat ceiling) – but as there are no shafts running the whole height of the wall the three storeys remain isolated from each other. The longitudinal emphasis carries the day and the effect of an overall soaring to great heights is still to come.

put a circular dome over a square plan – supported on four arches and four piers – can all this massive masonry be dispensed with and the plan opened out into surrounding areas – aisles, apses and so on. But when we try to put a dome over a square plan we find a triangular space is left at each corner, and this must be bridged. This problem was not solved immediately. Experiments were made through the centuries. One example is that of SS Sergius and Bacchus in Constantinople *(plate 22)*. This church

is designed with its dome over a central octagon. This is a com-
promise. It gives eight triangular spaces to be bridged, one at
each corner of the octagon but they are, of course, smaller than
if the plan had been a square. The picture also shows two of the
eight arches on each side of the octagon, and how the subordinate
parts of the plan – mainly a surrounding aisle in this case – open
out from the central area. This gave interest, complexity and
mystery; it also gave the domed, central area a dominant and

Plate 52
Near FLORENCE
San Miniato al Monte

It is not accidental that Renaissance architecture should have originated, at the beginning of the fifteenth century, in Florence. Throughout the Middle Ages, the city had like Rome, preserved its links with Late Antique and Early Christian tradition. The continued vitality of this heritage is perhaps best seen in the series of buildings raised in the eleventh and early twelfth centuries, of which the little church of San Minato al Monte is the masterpiece. Its main features are those of the Early Christian basilica: nave and two lower aisles, semicircular apse with mosaic decoration, open roofing. The diversity of the column capitals attests the old practice in church building of using spolia, *fragments taken from antique edifices.*

In other respects, however, San Miniato is a product of its time. The vast hall-like crypt which raises the level of the choir recalls similar constructions in contemporary Romanesque; so do the transverse arches spanning the nave at three-bay intervals and interrupting its flow towards the east end. The treatment of the walls, on the other hand, is quite original: white marble revetments with geometrical patterns – lines, squares, circles and so forth – inlaid in blue-black. The tonal effects are remarkable: black and white, combined with the red of the apsidal mosaic and the brown of the roof beams. It is noteworthy that the variety of the marble patterns does not, in any way, affect the structural clarity of the

unifying effect on the building as a whole.

In the end this problem of putting a circular dome over a square plan was fully solved by means of a device called the 'pendentive'. We can see a pendentive very clearly in the picture of Hagia Sophia, Constantinople *(plate 24)*. The central area of this huge church is a square with a big arch on each of the four sides. Above these four arches is the circular dome. It is supported on pendentives. Each of the four pendentives may be regarded as

interior. Entirely flat, attempting no trompe l'oeil, *they enrich the wall surface but also preserve its solidity, while their disposition harmonises with structural elements. This respect for the* ratio of *architecture looks foward to the Renaissance, and so San Miniato, together with other Florentine buildings in the same style, represents what is known as a Proto-Renaissance.*

a triangular slice of dome.

Geometrically, therefore, in the end, the answer was fairly simple, but only when it was mastered was the way open to the building of the world's great domes – Byzantine, Renaissance, Baroque. Sancta Sophia (AD 527) was the central church of the Byzantine style – one of the great churches of the world, giving us the greatest unbroken floor space in the world. In fact the central square was in effect doubled; on two sides additional areas opened

Plate 51
GLOUCESTER
Cathedral

Plate 52
Near FLORENCE
San Miniato Al Monte

Plate 53
LUCCA
San Michele

Its political connection with the Holy Roman Empire opened Northern Italy (Lombardy) in the Romanesque and Gothic periods to the influence of German architecture. Many borrowings are in evidence but not wholesale copying. To the elements taken over belongs probably the eaves gallery, a low arcade with a narrow passage engaged in the upper reaches of external walls, which first occurs about 1080 in the chancel of Speyer Cathedral. It then appears in the chancel, nave and façade of the Cathedral of Modena (begun in 1099) and again in the Cathedrals of Piacenza, Cremona, Ferrara and Parma (all begun in the first half of the twelfth century). From there it seems to have found its way to Central Italy, to Pisa and Lucca, where it achieved its finest and most elaborate form.

The façade of San Michele in Foro at Lucca (twelfth – thirteenth century), closely akin to that of the powerful Cathedral of Pisa, presents this feature in a lavish display. While the compact wall of the portal zone remains clearly visible behind the blind arcade of classical simplicity which continues along the side walls, the upper storeys are masked by a veritable screen in which four tiers of columns and openings between them make up a filigree texture of light and shadow. The wall and windows behind can at best be surmised. The effect of variety and liveliness is enhanced by the treatment of the colonnettes: they are decorated with mosaic, a common practice in Italy at the time, which gives them the appearance of sculpture, or

out of it, and these in turn were covered in semi-domes. Again, all round the main central area were aisles from which one could, through screens of intervening columns, see vistas right across the church. This is a building to which all Roman and Byzantine engineering had been leading, one to which all later Byzantine churches owe their being.

The Byzantine builder was concerned mainly with the interior, with the setting for ritual and with those solemn caverns benathe

*else twisted and knotted, as though made of rope. The narrow
courses above each tier are covered with fantastic animal shapes,
carrying no doubt, like the creatures appearing on Romanesque capitals, a precise meaning for contemporaries which is today largely lost.
This painterly and plastic richness does not, however, conceal the
overall clarity of the structure. The outline of the façade which
reflects the layout of the interior has the compactness of an ancient
temple. The galleries are sharply marked off from each other by
sturdy cornices. There can be no doubt that the heritage of Antiquity
is alive here just as much as in the products of the Florentine Proto-
Renaissance (plate 52).*

the domes. He hardly bothered himself, as did the Baroque architects centuries later, with the external effect of his dome. Michelangelo or Wren went to great lengths to create a skyline for the
city, putting their domes high on drums where no external abutment was possible – such domes had to be actually chained in
at the base – and then setting cupolas on top of them solely for
effect. The Byzantine building had a different intention. The dome
was a means to an end – the roofing over and enclosure of a

Plate 54
VENICE
San Marco

The eleventh century, which saw Romanesque achieve full maturity in Germany, France, England, and also Italy, witnessed in Venice the flowering of an entirely different style, that of Byzantium. Through its lively trade with the Orient, the rich and powerful maritime Republic had become a Byzantine emporium and almost a bridgehead of the Eastern Empire, more sensitive to its influence than any other region in the West. When the church of the city's patron, St Mark, was destroyed by fire, and the present structure raised, both the local architectural tradition and the not too distant Romanesque were neglected for a Byzantine model, the old and venerable Church of the Apostles in Constantinople, dating from Justinian's time (destroyed in 1463).

The plan of San Marco (begun in 1063, dedicated in 1093) is that of the Greek Cross with domes on pendentives over its centre and four arms. Mosaics with gold ground on surfaces of wall and vault lend to the interior, as in Byzantine churches, an atmosphere of intense awe. A lighter, lively prelude to this solemnity is offered by the façade with its Oriental profusion of ornament. One hardly notices that the groundfloor with its five apse-like, recessed portals is a product of the twelfth century showing strong Romanesque elements. These are revealed only by closer scrutiny: in the middle portal, for instance, in the graduated arch or in the reliefs with the signs of the zodiac and the labours of the months. In comparison

big space. Since Byzantine influence in Constantinople extended into the Mohammedan era we can see very well in, for instance, the Mosque of Sulaimān I *(plate 30)* what a large Byzantine exterior was like. Arches, buttresses, semi-domes and minor domes all pile up – like a mass of bubbles – to a central point, while the thrust of the main dome is ultimately conveyed to earth far from its starting point.

This Byzantine system of construction, like any other, produced

*the upper storey, set back a little, shows clearer evidence of the
Romanesque preference for bold effects of plasticity and mass with
its surfaces framed by a broad blind arcade. However, details are
dominated by the sumptuous and festive impression of the whole
to which the ogee extrados of the upper arches, each crowned by a
figure, and the flag-like canopies of the tabernacles contribute in an
important degree. They are fifteenth century Gothic additions.*

a corresponding system of decoration. That system, like the dome
itself, was a development of Roman methods. The great halls of
the Thermae and of other large Roman interiors were – as we
have seen – of mass construction with decoration of a covering
nature: paint, marble, mosaic. (We may set all this in opposition
to Greek or Gothic where there are no larger masses but, rather,
a multiplicity of columns, and where the structure is not so much
'decorated' as actually carved into, so as to emphasise function,

Plate 53
LUCCA
San Michele

Plate 54
VENICE
San Marco

Plate 55
MONREALE
Cathedral

Sicily, ruled successively in the early Middle Ages by Byzantine Greeks, Saracens and Normans, evolved under the Norman kings (1130–1189) a remarkable artistic synthesis out of its composite heritage. This is strikingly exemplified in the choir of the Cathedral of Monreale, the masterpiece of the period (begun in 1174). The Romanesque tendency to articulate exterior walls with blind arcading is here modified by an Islamic delight in covering wall surfaces with a carpet of ornament. As a result the Romanesque element does not come into its own: the wall is not resolved into a system of sharp lights and shadows but preserves its compactness under the flat ornament. Also Islamic are the interlacing pointed arches rising from slim colonnettes which are crowned with leaf capitals all' antica. *Finally the mosaic embroidery in the archivolts, the horizontal bands, and the circular shields are likewise of Islamic derivation. Comparison with entirely Moslem works (compare plate 28) shows how close the kinship is.*

i.e. the fluted Greek column, or the moulded Gothic mullion or vaulting rib.) The two glories of Byzantine art are its greatest structural feature and the decoration thereof – the dome and mosaic.

Mosaic is made from thousands of tiny cubes of coloured glass or marble, each less than half-an-inch across. A portion of the surface to be treated is cemented over, then each little cube is pressed into the wet cement with the thumb, all to a preconceived design. Like all arts mosaic must be designed with an under-standing of the medium; any attempt to imitate the natural realism of painting is doomed to failure. (That is equally true of stained glass.) Mosaic, when seen near to, should be almost incomprehensible – so broad and simple should the drawing be. It should come into its own only when seen from far off. This means that the right place for it is high up on the under surface of domes and arches high above one's head. Also, in some mysterious way,

Plate 56
CHARTRES
Cathedral

There is an old French saying that to build a perfect cathedral towers should be taken from Chartres, façade from Paris, nave from Amiens and sculpture from Rheims. Towers from Chartres . . . He who has seen these cathedrals, the first magnificent flower of French Gothic, will appreciate the choice.

The two Chartres towers have a peculiar charm which derives from the uneven height of the spires, a feature all the more striking as Amiens and Rheims, though at first intended to have spires, in the end never had them (see plate 57). In Chartres the unevenness is the result of piecemeal construction. The south spire, sturdy and enriched by carving only at its base, was put up in the thirteenth century according to the original plan; the dissolute late Gothic of its northern partner is a product of the sixteenth century.

This direct juxtaposition of old and new, which today seems so astonishing, is a fine proof of the originality and strength of medieval architecture: with a sovereign disregard for historical consistency or even mere symmetry, it knew unerringly how to bring together in a tense yet indissoluble harmony formal types that were apparently irreconcilable. The Chartres spires are a prime example. The same applies to the façade. The lower part of the flanking towers with their powerful buttresses rising to full height belongs to the Romanesque structure of Bishop Fulbert which was burnt down in 1194 and immediately replaced by the present church (1194 to

the broad, crude, stiff and archaic draftsmanship of the mosaicist is very appropriate to the solemn saints and apostles of the Eastern Church.

Mosaic, composed as it is of such very small cubes, is really just as much a 'covering' material as paint or plaster. This is emphasised when the mosaic is allowed to run round corners rather than being framed in by mouldings as if it were a picture. As we see it not only in Hagia Sophia but in the little tomb of

1220); the towers were then given their Gothic windows. Again, the lower middle part of the façade is Romanesque. Originally the three portals with their celebrated statuary stood further back; after the fire they were brought forward and made flush with the towers, and a Gothic rose window and Gothic gallery of kings were added above.

Galla Placidia and in the Church of San Vitale, both in Ravenna *(plates 21 and 23)*, the mosaic runs on, almost as if molten, over the curved surfaces of dome, arch and pendentive. The small windows – originally filled with alabaster, not glass – which are almost the only windows possible in this massive Byzantine architecture, cast only an occasional gleam of sunlight onto the mosaic, so that the occasional glitter gives life to the otherwise sombre interior.

228

Plate 55
MONREALE
Cathedral

Plate 56
CHARTRES
Cathedral

Plate 57
PARIS
Cathedral of Notre Dame

With Chartres, Rheims and Amiens, Notre Dame represents the first climax, never surpassed, of French Gothic. Begun in 1163 with the choir and completed in the second half of the thirteenth century with the west front, it is the eldest of these four royal sisters. Neither inside nor outside does it achieve the beauty and minute elegance of Rheims or Amiens. But both in structure and plan it is, if austere and unemphatic, unmistakably Gothic.

The aim of Gothic builders to make the interior no longer a sum of self-contained parts arranged round the opening of the crossing tower but a dynamic unity developing from west to east is evident in Notre Dame. The Romanesque crossing tower has disappeared and the vault under it has been integrated with those of the nave and the choir to form one continuous whole. The unity of the interior is reflected outside. From the monumental opening note of the towers the body of the building flows to the final semi-circle of the choir, uninterrupted either by the delicate turret which replaces the crossing tower or the relatively short wings of the transept.

Moreover, the whole of the exterior is characterised by the typically French concern for clarté *and* raison *to the neglect of emotional religiosity such as it finds expression for instance in the mighty towers of German High Gothic. Vertical elements, for example the tower buttresses, are opposed by powerful horizontals which check their upward thrust and bring about a remarkably un-Gothic*

The whole thing is a marriage between Roman engineering and eastern mysticism – a marriage brought about by Greek artists. Outwardly it is as different from the art of classical Greece as it well could be .... nevertheless it has the same genius, the same unity.

calm. Also characteristic is the absence of spires, which is quite intentional and not in the least an indication of unfinished work. Finally, another illustration of the pursuit of clarity, the roof is sharply set off from the rest of the building.

In 1210 the predecessor of the Gothic Cathedral, a Carolingian edifice, built under Louis the Pious and subsequently altered, was burnt down. Exactly a year later the foundation stone was laid for a new church, whose architectural magnificence was to match the traditional honour of witnessing the coronations of the French monarchs, and which Charles VIII was to call at the end of the fifteenth century the 'noblest among all churches of royal France'. As was customary in medieval church building, work began on the chancel, planned by Jean d'Orbais. In 1241 it was ready for dedication. With ambulatory and radiating chapels, opening on a relatively narrow transept, it is a typical product of French Cathedral Gothic, though, strictly speaking, not an original one. It is anticipated in French Romanesque chancels such as that of St Sernin at Toulouse (plate 46).

This kinship between the earlier and the later serves to bring out the differences between them. In the Romanesque version the component parts – the main body of the chancel, the ambulatory and the several radiating chapels – are distinct and autonomous, and the relation of part to whole is immediately intelligible. In the Gothic structure the chapels have been knit together with the ambulatory. The composition of the whole is not easy to analyse. It is further obscured, veiled as it were, by the framework of flying buttresses, doubled in Rheims, the celebrated Gothic device for

Romanesque

The decline and fall of the Roman Empire was a more complicated process and a more prolonged one than even Gibbon has suggested. It was never complete. Apart altogether from the fact that Rome spawned the Eastern or Byzantine Empire, certain institutions, customs, laws, pagan rites and fragments of culture have lived on. True, there was a date when the Legions had to be withdrawn from such distant outposts as Britain; there was a date when the

containing the side thrust of the high vault, canalising it outwards and 'earthing' it.

The buttresses are crowned by pinnacles (their bodies hollowed out to receive statues), whose airy vertical accents lighten the mass of the structure and lend it some of the upward drive that dominates Gothic interiors. The drive is not, however, given free rein, as in the case of German churches: the eaves of the chapels and the main body of the chancel are surmounted by a wide horizontal band of arcades respectively pierced and blind, which holds the ascending movement in check.

A special feature of the chancel of Rheims may be noticed. It is here that bar tracery makes its first appearance. In contrast to the earlier plate tracery in which the ground is solid wall and the pattern consists of holes punched in it, in Rheims it is the large window openings that are the ground and thin moulded bars introduced into them that make up the pattern. The invention was not prompted in the first instance by aesthetic considerations but by the need to subdivide the ever larger area for glazing.

postal services no longer reached Spain, and when the water stopped running in the aqueducts; there was a day when Gothic or Teutonic chieftains themselves assumed the purple. But there was never a time when men admitted that the Empire had ended.

Through the centuries – until Christmas Day AD 800 when Charlemagne was crowned Emperor of the West and 'The First Europe' was born – the tribal territories of the tributary peoples were slowly organising themselves under the tutelage of the

Plate 57
PARIS
Cathedral of Nôtre Dame

Plate 58
RHEIMS
Cathedral

Plate 59
BOURGES
Cathedral

The Cathedral of Bourges (begun about 1195, completed including West front by about 1270), is one of the most original creations of early French Gothic; of a period, that is, in which the principles of the new style, though making headway against those of the old, had not finally dislodged them. And it is precisely here in Bourges, somewhat remote in the provincialitij of Berry from the great architectural events occurring in the Ile de France, that the old and the new frequently appear side by side in unresolved contradiction. Thus on the one hand the powerful, five-aisled structure realizes the Gothic principle of a unified interior to the extent of having no transept and allowing its nave to flow uninterruptedly from west to east. On the other hand, however, the vaulting of the nave is sexpartite, a retrograde feature, of whose space-dividing effect we spoke in connection with the Cathedral of Laon (plate 49). And, as in that edifice, the system of responds – groups of alternately three and five – which follows from the uneven distribution of the ribs, breaks up the uniformity of the wall above the arcade and gives it a horizontal rhythm. True, the disruptive tendency of this articulation is much weaker than in Laon. It is limited by the height of the arcade whose uniform pillars rise to almost half the distance from ground to vault and thus leave the responds little room for their independent effects.

The violent upward movement of the arcades, expressed in the piers

Universal Church and under the civilising influence of monastic orders, until in the end they emerged as the succession states, as Feudal Christendom.

The architecture of those 'lost centuries' is one which bridges the yawning gap between the Roman Thermae and the Gothic cathedrals. It is the architecture that we call 'Romanesque'. It is the standing proof – however often we may contrast the outward and stylistic differences of this style and that – that European

*and continued up to the vault by the groups of responds, is in
accordance with the Gothic principle of vertical accents in the articulation of the interior, both the space and the shell enclosing it. But
in Bourges the principle is not fully realised. The nave is too broad
to ascend to the vault in a truly Gothic manner, along steep and
slender lines – all the more so as the enormous arcades opening like
portals into the high aisles bring these into play as sideward extensions of the nave, thus assimilating it to the hall type of interior.
In this way the upward drive fails to achieve the relentlessness
characteristic of fully developed Gothic.*

architecture really is a unity, a variety of beads on a single string.
Romanesque architecture really was Roman-like in that it carried
further both the massive structure and the cross-vault of Rome,
in that its sign-manual was the semi-circular arch *(plates 39 to 47)*
and in that its builders really believed that they were building
Roman temples for the new religion. For all that it was in Romanesque that the great idea of the Gothic cathedral plan was
developed, creating structural problems for which absolute solu-

Plate 60
AMIENS
Cathedral

In 1218 the Romanesque Cathedral, the fourth in succession, was destroyed by fire. Two years later work was begun on a new church, a powerful Gothic structure. The ambitious patron, Bishop Evrart de Fouilloy, intended that it should be a unique architectural achievement surpassing Paris, Chartres and Rheims, the last-mentioned begun less than ten years before. And indeed under the initial direction of an architect of genius, Robert de Luzarches, a building was raised in less than fifty years that answered this exacting requirement not only by its size (27,627 square feet of roofed surface, 784,800 cubic feet of enclosed space, becoming thereby the largest French Cathedral) but by the sweep and clarity of its conception, a rapid and brilliant climax in the development of the new style. It is as though the architect had extracted from what was already in existence or under construction the various components of the Gothic ideal of structure and space which he then proceeded to combine in an entirely original manner and with admirable consistency. Nowhere else are the characteristic features of Gothic displayed to greater advantage and nowhere else is the change from Romanesque more forcefully brought home.

Gone is the breadth of interior found in Laon (plate 49) and which still remained in Paris and Bourges (plate 59). The steep ascent of the nave, intensified by the articulation of the walls, produces a soaring effect of compelling beauty. The evenly distributed responds

tions were found ultimately only by Gothic builders.

The Romanesque style covered the world of Western Christendom – France, Spain, England and what we now call Germany. The Romanesque builders were princes, bishops and abbots in half-barbaric lands where learning and art were wholly in the hands of the Church. Outside the Church men were simple and illiterate, usually cruel and bestial or else – perhaps in revulsion against the world round them – gloomy, superstitious and pietistic.

243

start from the ground and, given added momentum by the high arcades, guide the eye to the distant vaults which seem to float in mid-air. The ribs transmit the movement from below to the vertex. Nor is the forceful upward drive broken by the triforium. As a separate storey it was found to strike a discordant note: while in the nave it is still the usual arcaded gallery, a zone of shadow hollowed out in the wall, in the later transept and chancel its outer side is glazed, thus integrating it into the vertically accented system of fenestration. The paramount aspiration upwards is thus brought about not merely by the distribution of accents, but by an actual disembodiment of the fabric, by relieving the wall of the downward pull of solid stone. The same consistency is apparent in the horizontal unification of the interior. The crossing is no longer, as in Romanesque structures, a tower shaft separating nave from chancel and one wing of the transept from the other: its ceiling is level with the high vault and an integral part of it. The sexpartite vault with the dome-like centring has been replaced by narrow, oblong bays. They do not arrest the eye but on the contrary lead it on in a steady movement from compartment to compartment. This, together with uniformity and even distribution of members along the sides, results in a unified flow from the entrance to the polygonal chancel, to the high altar, where rest and fulfilment are found.

In that lost Europe there was energy and strength and faith, very little sweetness or light. That world was reflected, as always, in its architecture. Romanesque is, in the main, an architecture of thick walls, massive piers, heavy arches and small windows – dark and cumbersome, but also impressive, courageous and not without pathos.

So far as the plan of the greater churches was concerned the Romanesque style took over and developed the very simple plan

Plate 59
BOURGES
Cathedral

Plate 60
AMIENS
Cathedral

Plate 61
COLOGNE
Cathedral

In the long run not even Germany with its conservative tendencies could resist the forceful progress of French Cathedral Gothic. The first German building to adopt the new style fully and without reservation was the Cathedral of Cologne. In 1247 the Cathedral Chapter decided that the old Carolingian church, a powerful two-choir and two-transept structure, should be dismantled and replaced. The foundation stone for the new church was laid in 1248 and the work of construction began, following the design of a Master Gerhard, in sections so that religious functions should not be interrupted (the old nave was retained until the end of the Middle Ages). The chancel was dedicated in 1322. It is the only entirely medieval part of the building. Only in the nineteenth century, though according to old plans, were the nave and the celebrated two-tower West front raised to their full height over an earlier substructure.

The patrons as well as Gerhard, the master mason, and his successors were bent on equalling if not surpassing, the wonderful French achievement. Cologne is rightly named in one breath with Amiens because there is no doubt that the magnificent Picard Cathedral was taken as a model. But the kinship between the two works is like that of sisters who despite the many traits they share yet have each a distinct personality. Cologne is inspired by Amiens but does not follow it slavishly, indeed in many respects departs

of the Early Christian basilica. The builders kept the long nave and reserved it for the people – the common people who stood or knelt on its stone paving. But, in various other ways, the Romanesque builders developed the eastern limb for their great choral services – plain-song and then, later, Gregorian chanting – and for a ritual inconceivable to the primitive Christian. Not yet do we find the very long chancels and presbyteries – as long as the nave itself – such as we see in, say, the Gothic cathedrals of

from the model. Remarkable above all is the dogmatic rigour in the arrangement of the interior, disciplined to the last detail and pruned of all irrelevances and contradictions still tolerated to some extent in Amiens. Thus Cologne does not accept the sturdy core of the four-shaft composite column, out of harmony with the prevailing fine division into separate members, but transforms the whole support into a cluster of shafts. The string-courses which at Amiens run across the shafts at each storey, bind them to the wall and interrupt them horizontally, have been eliminated. The vertical members rise from ground to vault completely unimpeded. The triforium which even in the chancel and transept of Amiens retains a certain character of its own has here, following the more advanced example of St Denis, been brought entirely into line with the clerestory windows and, through its tracery, linked with them to form a whole.

In sum, Cologne surpasses Amiens in formal clarity though at the expense of warmth and personal character. The typical and the regular dominate throughout with a somewhat unprepossessing rigidity. However all this is concealed by the atmosphere that suffuses the interior. It comes here as elsewhere from the multi-coloured stained glass which stretches like a glittering film over the structural skeleton. It transmutes the inflowing light into an unreal luminosity and the space within becomes a world of its own.

Salisbury *(plate 68)* or Exeter *(plate 69)*, but we do find that the semi-circular apse of the early basilica – which had been big enough only for an altar and half-a-dozen clergy – has now grown out of all recognition, as at Cologne *(plate 40)* or Worms *(plate 41)*. At Toulouse *(plate 46)* it has begun to sprout not only transepts – those side wings which were to be the arms of the cruciform plan – but also a ring of surrounding chapels, clearly capable of development into the glorious chevet of chapels that

Plate 62
RATISBON
Cathedral

While French architecture remained faithful to the Gothic cathedral type and innovated little between the late thirteenth and the fifteenth century, German episcopal and town parish churches already in the thirteenth century show a disinclination to follow the example of Cologne (plate 61) and accept French models. They go their own way in ground plan and structure without, however, evolving a unified type. For instance, in the Cathedral of Ratisbon (built between c. 1270 and 1325), the chancel has no ambulatory or radiating chapels. It is a single apse though the articulation of its walls, as of those of the later nave, is modelled on French examples and on Cologne. The comfortable breadth of the interior, enhanced by the shallow, very obtusely pointed transverse arches, deprives it of the soaring effect of Cologne, even though the shafts offer forceful lines of ascent. A definite wish to restrain the upward drive seems to assert itself: while the chancel triforium is still glazed, in the nave it has recovered its back wall and hence its distinctness as a storey while reversing the trend towards the disembodiment of the fabric. This reversal is generally in evidence at the end of the thirteenth century. The articulation of the triforium and clerestory stage is simplified and their character as parts of an enclosing wall is maintained. In this respect the Freiburg Minster, (after 1260), for example, or the Cathedrals of Halberstadt (after 1252) and Magdeburg (after 1272) are

we find in the French cathedrals, as for instance at Rheims *(plate 58)*. We note however that as we look down the long perspective of Vézelay *(plate 44)* or St Etienne, Caen *(plate 48)* that we are looking down a Romanesque nave, with a rhythm of semi-circular arches, to a distant glimpse of a later Gothic channel, with a rhythm of pointed arches.

Apart from the carving of capitals or bands of rather archaic ornament (elementary zig-zags etc.) Romanesque architecture can

more thorough-going than Ratisbon: the triforium is done away with altogether and the wall between the arcade and the clerestory is left as a plain surface.

hardly be said to have had a decorative *system*. Such richness and orchestration of the masonry as there was grew directly out of the solution of structural problems, rather than from any consciously applied decoration. It was what we would now call a 'functional' style. In any case the years from, say, 800 to 1100 are not an era wherein men had either the wealth, skill or inclination to make their buildings ornate. Ornament was kept, rather, for smaller things such as the illuminated initial or the

Plate 61
COLOGNE
Cathedral

Plate 62
RATISBON
Cathedral

Plate 63
STRASBOURG
Cathedral

The tendency towards refining the wall into a trellis work of delicate tracery is just as evident without as within Gothic churches. Without it achieves its greatest triumphs in façades and their towers, producing an often superabundant wealth of ornament. The finest and most mature example is, without doubt, the west front of the Cathedral of Strasbourg, more exactly the entrance and the gigantic rose window. Only these belong to the extant but otherwise unexecuted design of Erwin von Steinbach which provides for a façade and two towers with spires entirely covered by tracery. The lower part of the façade begun in 1277 (the rose window dates from 1360) gives some idea of what Erwin had in mind. Practically no surface is left undifferentiated; the buttresses are decorated with blind tracery while the recessed portions above the portals have, standing free in front of them, open-work tracery of lace-like refinement. The space intervening between this delicate veil and the wall enhances the variegated play of forms and of light and shadow, conferring upon the whole an indescribable, almost unreal lightness.

chalice. Buildings reflected the dour asceticism of the early monastic orders.

Nevertheless, when the Western Church applied the massive structure and round arch of Rome to the columned nave of the early basilica, something happened which in fact produced a new architecture. First, everything was bigger, heavier, stronger, more masculine than in the early basilicas. Style apart, we may well contrast, say, Vézelay *(plate 44)* or Angoulême *(plate 45)* with Sta Sabina *(plate 19)*. Secondly, the blank wall between the nave arcade – i.e. the arcade opening through from nave to aisle – and the sill of the clerestory windows above, which had in Early Christian times been painted or treated with mosaic, were now often pierced with arches. These arches, unlike the clerestory windows above, opened out not into the exterior but into the dark space above the aisle vault, and below the lean-to roof over that vault. We can best understand this by comparing

Plate 64
ULM
Minster

In German Gothic the two-tower façade elaborated in France is relatively rare. Town parish churches particularly, put up by the burghers in rivalry with the cathedrals — the responsibility of the bishops — which they often exceeded in size, showed a marked preference for the single tower front. Strictly speaking this is not a façade but a monumentalised portal consisting, as in Ulm and Freiburg, of a vestibule surmounted by one mighty tower. According to the design of Ulrich von Ensingen who began the tower of Ulm in 1392, this was to be of colossal height outdoing everything so far achieved and thus satisfying the ambition of the proud burghers of Ulm for a monument demonstrating their power, riches and exalted view of their position. However, at the end of the Middle Ages, when the original enthusiasm and material means had ebbed away, the enormous undertaking was left only half finished. About 1460 the structure was carried up to the base of the octagon (341 feet). The rest, that is the octagon and the spire, were added in the eighteen-eighties, not in accordance with old designs and in a somewhat unimaginative brand of Gothic. The old and the new are clearly distinguishable by the varying colour of the stone.

The Ulm tower, with its 530 feet, is the highest stone church tower in the world, and even though it is not entirely medieval its structure gives a fair idea of German towers of the Gothic period. In contrast to French practice, the square top was not favoured, and spires

two examples of early Romanesque where it is not done, Alpirsbach *(plate 38)* or Vézelay *(plate 44)*, with two examples, St Etienne, Caen *(plate 48)* or Peterborough *(plate 50)*, where it is done. This is the 'dark storey'. The arches show light against the deep shadow behind them; they are thus in contrast with the clerestory above, where the arches or tracery are dark against light. This 'dark storey' is called the triforium. It provided a walk-way and a place from which one could look down on the service far below. Its

259

appear regularly, forming the climax of the narrowing by stages of the tower shaft. Covered entirely, as here in Ulm, by blind or open-work tracery they shoot up, like pertrified fountains, in an unbroken jet into the sky.

function, however, was not important; it arrived almost of itself when once the wall in front of the aisle lean-to roof was pierced. Then its architectural value was seen and exploited.

Immediately this gives us a new aesthetic in more ways than one. The interior space is now not so much dominated by an all-embracing vault or dome, as in Roman or Byzantine architecture, as by a treatment of the wall involving range upon range of arcades — the main nave arcade, the triforium above that, then

Plate 63
STRASBOURG
Cathedral

Plate 64
ULM
Minster

Plate 65
LUBECK
Church of the Virgin

Brick (clay pressed into moulds and burnt), once the favourite building material of the Romans, was entirely forgotten by early medieval masons, who used dressed quarry stone. It is only when the stoneless plains of North and North-East Germany were opened up by colonisation that the use of brick was revived. The growth of numerous towns to which successful trade, especially overseas trade, soon brought power, prosperity and renown, created the need for monumental architecture. The need could not be met in the same way as elsewhere because the only stone materials available were granite driftblocks from the Ice Age, hard, difficult to dress, and in any case rare. Brick provided the solution. Recommended perhaps by the example of North Italy, it became the favourite, almost the only, building material in these northern and eastern regions of Germany.

From the thirteenth century onwards many brick buildings, most often churches, were constructed, yielding neither in size nor in dignity to stone edifices yet with a distinct formal idiom of their own. This sprang from the nature of the material. Brick cannot be wrought like natural stone: it will not stand piercing, shaping into delicate fillets or tapering to fine points; also, more brittle, it is less resistant.

Since brick structures could not aspire to the fine-membered elegance of stone building, they developed instead a harsh, almost uncouth,

the clerestory. Arcading then becomes a motif for its own sake, almost an obsession, as we see it externally where it has no function, at San Michele, Lucca *(plate 53)*.

These ranges of arches, however, are not just surface decoration as were, for example, the arcades on the exterior of the Colosseum. They have thickness, depth and structural importance. The undersides – soffits – of the arches as well as the wall thickness are not only revealed; they matter more than the wall surface itself.

265

yet impressive language of massive walls, heavy often undifferentiated piers, and powerfully spanned arches. This can be discerned even in the Church of the Virgin at Lübeck (begun in the second half of the thirteenth century) which, with its lofty nave, high arcades and large clerestory windows, with responds shooting up uninterruptedly to the vaults and clustered piers in the choir, was clearly an attempt to emulate Western stone Gothic — not without an admission of inferiority as regards the building material: for the brick is masked by a coat of plaster with an ashlar pattern painted on it. Only where the red of the brick contributes to the articulation of particular features, as, for instance, in the responds, has it been allowed to declare itself. On the other hand the indigenous character of North German brick Gothic (Backsteingotik) *is exemplified not so much in the choir as in the somewhat later nave with its sturdy rectangular piers.*

In fact, what at first seemed a handicap of Romanesque – massiveness – is now being cut into and exploited so as to become, after all, a decorative system – at least in effect.

Aesthetically, too, these ranging arches, or system of arcades, were exploited in other directions. Penetration, depth, the perspective and vista *through* the wall, from one part of the church to another, as at Gloucester *(plate 51)* become all important. Externally, too, this arcading becomes the insignia of the style.

Plate 66
LANDSHUT
St Martin

While in France and England, Late Gothic (fourteenth and fifteenth centuries) is conservative in the fundamentals of structure and plan, and change is discernible only in the decoration, in the growing complexity of capitals, arches, vault ribbing and window tracery, Germany in the same period begins to turn more and more towards a new structural type – the hall church in which the aisles rise to the same height as the nave. The type occurs already in the Romanesque period, especially in the South of France and in Westphalia, but is ousted almost completely by the Gothic basilican cathedral. It reappears suddenly at the end of the fourteenth century in South and South East Germany and holds the field until the beginning of the Renaissance.

The Church of St Martin at Landshut, begun by Hans Stethaimer in 1392 and completed about 1460, inaugurates what is known as German Sondergotik. The main body of the church, as against the choir, has a nave and two aisles, all of equal height. The hexagonal pillars connected by arcades divide the nave from the aisles; succeeding each other rapidly at one metre intervals they accelerate the movement eastward. But the eye, deprived of its blinkers by the absence of upper walls, tends to wander sideways into the aisles where it is attracted by the high, bright windows, and recognises in the vaults the same system of ribbing as in the nave. The interior as a whole is no longer a compound of distinct parts but one spatial

Whether the arches are part of the structure and function, as in doors and windows, or whether they are just a kind of structural treatment of the wall, the ghost of this nave arcade, triforium and clerestory, all come through to haunt the exterior, or – to put it more simply – to find external expression, as at Cologne *(plate 40)* or Worms *(plate 41)*.

The division of the Romanesque church into three main horizontal parts – nave arcade, triforium and clerestory – was of

unit merely interrupted by colonnades. This unification of space, suggested rather than stated in Landshut, will become fully explicit in later hall structures, in fifteenth century choirs and early sixteenth-century hall churches in the Erzgebirge; the arcade above the pillars will disappear and the ribbing will run on into the aisles thus unifying the ceiling.

St Martin is a brick structure and, as in the Church of the Virgin in Lübeck (plate 65), the 'artificial substitute' conceals itself under a coat of paint with a stone block pattern.

enormous importance for the future. Variations upon this theme are the basis of the design of the Gothic cathedrals. In the exterior of Notre Dame, Paris *(plate 57)* we see the importance given to the clerestory (glimpsed above the trees); in the interior of Bourges or Amiens *(plates 59 and 60)* it is to the nave arcade that height has been given; while at Cologne *(plate 61)* it is once again the clerestory that dominates. Salisbury *(plate 68)*, fine as it is, comes perilously near dullness, no one of the three parts is

Plate 65
LUBECK
Church of the Virgin

Plate 66

LANDSHUT

St. Martin

Plate 67
LINCOLN
Cathedral

The reception of Gothic in England, hastened no doubt by the Cistercians, had already occurred in the late twelfth century, at a time when Germany was still fully immersed in Romanesque and when even in its country of origin, France, the new style had not achieved a conscious unity. What English masons learnt from the Continent or French masons brought with them was not a fully-fledged system but the first results of gropings towards as yet uncertain aims, a stage of development represented, for instance, by the cathedrals of Laon (plate 49) and Sens. This was of decisive importance because, as an incomplete growth, the new style lent itself more readily to a re-working in terms of native English notions of form and space, which had already brought about a special version of Romanesque (see plates 50, 51). For all its dependence on the Continent, English Gothic shows from the beginning a distinct character which at least in the early stages (Early English), strikes one as a transposition into Gothic terms of what remains essentially English Romanesque.

The close links between Romanesque and early Gothic can be observed in the west front of Lincoln Cathedral. The edifice, a basilica with two transepts, was begun in 1192 to replace a damaged and partly dismantled Romanesque predecessor which had been completed only in the middle of the century. In the west front, however, considerable portions of the older structure were preserved:

given real domination. The related problem which Romanesque builders handed on to Gothic builders was that of taking a church thus functionally divided horizontally, while at the same time giving it aesthetically that vertical emphasis which was so expressive of Mediaeval aspiration. This will be referred to again when Gothic architecture is considered.

The thick walls of Romanesque solved almost automatically the great problem of all arcuated and vaulted building   that of

the pair of towers (added to in the fourteenth century) and the curious centre of the façade with its enormous arched recesses hollowed out in the plain masonry. This centre was simply kept and made part of a much wider frontal wall, the whole presenting an impressive screen which, contrary to all Continental usage, is structurally independent of the towers behind it. It seems as though the stretching out of the façade was intended to compensate for the stark verticality of the Romanesque recesses, especially as the added parts are completely covered with horizontally arranged rows of blind arcades. Verticals and horizontals oppose each other in sharp directness. But the opposition is not one between Gothic and Romanesque. The older portion of the façade already had similar rows of blind arcades over the side recesses (one has survived), so that the Gothic masons were here only imitators. The monotonous, wearying accumulation of identical elements is also common to Romanesque and Gothic arcadings. All this reflects formal principles which were to be a constant feature of English architecture: horizontal ranging and serial repetition.

thrust and counter-thrust. The wall itself is usually strong enough to receive the outward thrust of the main vault or of the nave arcade. If we look at our Romanesque exteriors *(plates 39 to 42)* we see no buttresses, only a flat pilaster or attached half-column – a kind of token indication of the point of the arch's thrust within. The moment the more scientific Gothic builder began to enlarge windows and pare away walls, then the wall can no longer act as if it were a buttress, and the buttress – including flying

274

Plate 68
SALISBURY
Cathedral

In its treatment of space and structure English Gothic parts company, from the outset, with French and general Continental practice. This can be shown by comparing, for instance, Amiens (plate 60) and Salisbury, contemporary almost to the year – both were begun in 1220 and finished in the 'sixties – yet belonging to different worlds. All that makes Amiens the archetype of French Cathedral Gothic – the slim, lofty interior rising to the distant vaults, the uniform movement of the nave towards its consummation in the choir apse, the walls refined into delicate trellis work or else transfigured into light as they become transparent sheets of glass – all this is lacking in Salisbury. Its interior is relatively wide and low but stretches a distance unequalled anywhere on the continent and, with no upward drive to balance it, length is easily the dominant dimension. The eye looks in vain for continuous lines of ascent supplied in continental Gothic by shafts running from ground to vault. Here the vaulting shafts have divorced themselves from arcade pillars thus obscuring the play of thrust and counterthrust. More in the nature of consoles, they have withdrawn to the spandrels of the gallery and, offering no guidance to the eye, seem to hang from the vaults rather than carry them. This emphatic disclaimer of verticality leaves free the two series of arches and supports formed by the main arcade and the gallery to engage in a joint movement towards the east – no doubt an intentional effect, further enhanced by a horizontal

buttress – appears as a structural and architectural feature in its own right, as at Paris *(plate 57)* or Rheims *(plate 58).*

Another problem arising from arch and vault building – as we saw in the case of Rome – was the making and erection of vast quantities of centring – that is, the temporary wooden supports for the arch, removable only when the final keystone is in position. The Roman division of their great halls into square bays – as opposed to a tunnel vault from end to end – had helped in that

distribution of colour accents resulting from the use of polished Purbeck marble for the attached shafts and capitals of the main arcade, the gallery colonnettes, the dwarf vaulting shafts, and the shafts of the clerestory.

Yet – an astonishing and typically English trait – this determined procession into depth, so carefully built up, is aimless. It does not come to rest and fulfilment in the semi-circle of a choir apse but hits a perpendicular wall, wells up against it and, its momentum spent, trickles out through the three-light upper window and the glass walls of the Lady Chapel adjoining the choir on the east. Thus the interior has no clear termination, it seems capable of being continued, and will become more so in later buildings when the east wall is converted into one enormous window.

Finally, a word about the articulation of the nave walls. It draws on Continental Gothic for its vocabulary but its grammar remains Romanesque. Comparison with a Norman structure like Gloucester (plate 51) reveals close similarities, for instance in the clerestory with its arcade screen and narrow passage in front of the windows. On the other hand the Romanesque emphasis on the sculptural qualities of mass and plasticity is replaced by an elegant, playfully light, draughtsmanlike linearism in individual elements and a sense of pattern in the grouping of them (e.g. the compound pillars of the main arcade and the gallery colonnettes).

it allowed the centring for one bay to be dismantled and used again in the next bay. The Romanesque builder, however, when he made his whole architecture one of arcades and arches in thick walls, faced this problem in an acute form. His solution was neat and highly architectural, even if its latent possibilities were left for exploitation by Gothic builders. We build an arch through a thick wall; the centring to support it must be as wide as the wall is thick – Aachen *(plate 34)* – but if, instead, we build

Plate 67
LINCOLN
Cathedral

Plate 68
SALISBURY
Cathedral

Plate 69
EXETER
Cathedral

In its further development English Gothic followed the path indicated for it in the first half of the thirteenth century by Early English works such as Lincoln and Salisbury (plates 67–8). Down to the fourteenth century the spatial articulation of the interior and the treatment of the wall surface remained substantially the same, innovation finding its scope in ornamental enrichment. How well justified the term 'Decorated' is for English High Gothic (1250–1340) can perhaps best be seen in the Cathedral of Exeter, one of the main works of the period. The choir, erected about 1280 or 1290, reveals an exuberant, almost overwhelming splendour. The walls have hardly any undifferentiated surface left. They have become magnificent arcade screens subdivided into a series of contiguous zones. The piers gather each sixteen shafts of reed-like slenderness and the profile of the arches sprung from them is broken up into innumerable mouldings, a gradation of delicate strokes. This preference for a multiple linearism in the contour of individual forms is apparant in every part of the interior but its finest product is the vault – a rich pattern of compartments created by a profusion of ribs.

All this does not obscure the horizontal emphasis which the comfortably broad structure shares with Salisbury (plate 68). True, the vaulting shafts reach down to the main arcade but they are not connected with the piers; they start immediately above from ornate,

our arch in a series of rings, each projecting slightly beyond the one below – St Etienne, Caen *(plate 48)* or Peterborough *(plate 50)* – then our centring need only support the lower ring during construction; the lower ring itself then acts as centring for the upper rings. Each ring of the arch – as we see in those same two examples – is then provided with a moulding or column to correspond to it in the pier below. Thus, through a purely practical attempt to reduce wooden centring, we have not only

281

gilded foliage corbels. Moreover the sheaves in which they are grouped are so slight that, in spite of the colour contrast with the wall, they do not assert themselves as verticals against the horizontal movement of the arcade and the triforium. The movement into depth is at its most concentrated in the vault at the vertex of which, like a ship's keel, a ridge rib thrusts forward. It gathers to itself the rib arches rising from the sides and draws the eye irresistibly towards the glistening glass wall of the gigantic east window.

lightened the structure, we have created a new kind of architecture – one of 'compound' piers and arches. This had immeasurable consequences. As the centuries pass the compound piers and arches of Romanesque become more complex until they become the richly moulded piers and arches of Gothic *(plates 61, 62 and 68)*. Greek architecture had been itself hardly carved at all; it was, rather, conceived as a setting for sculpture. Roman and Byzantine architecture had *applied* various forms of decoration to walls and

Among the most original achievements of English Gothic, and one of the most interesting types of spatial layout in architecture, are chapter houses, usually eight- or ten-sided, centrally planned structures whose interiors are singularly attractive. They served as places of assembly for monastic communities, and as many English cathedrals, unlike Continental ones, were not only episcopal churches but also abbeys attached to monasteries (hence the unusual length of choirs), chapter houses occur frequently. They could also be built for secular canons, and the earliest example, the decagonal chapter house of Lincoln (1220–1235), established the type for later ones. In the centre is a tall, slender, clustered column from which vaulting ribs shoot out like palm fronds from their stem. As they rise to the vault they spread out. This kind of vaulting must have been the model for the magnificent palm-vault as it appears, for instance, half a century later in the nave and choir of Exeter (plate 69).

The enrichment of the ceiling with innumerable linear elements indicates a tendency on the part of English Gothic to vary visual effects to a greater degree than is structurally required. The tendency is apparant everywhere else in the building, in the multiple mouldings of the arches, the clustered colonnettes, the shafts grouped in the window zone and those attached to the central pier. The Purbeck marble used for the shafts and colonnettes adds considerably by its colouring to the richness achieved by structural means.

vaults. Now, in Romanesque we see the birth of Gothic, an architecture in which the actual structure is carved and moulded – piers, arches, mullions, tracery, vaulting ribs. That is the essence of Gothic. It not only incorporates sculpture, it is itself sculpture.

Thus did Romanesque create a whole series of problems – the need for more daylight than was possible with those thick walls; a more scientific understanding of the vault and its abutment, the aesthetics of a masonic or carved building. Romanesque builders had begun to stumble upon solutions to these problems when the invention of the pointed arch with all its consequences – at St Denis, Chartres, Durham – suddenly created a more flexible, more precise and more scientific way of building – the style that we call 'Gothic'.

Plate 69
EXETER
Cathedral

Plate 70
LINCOLN
Cathedral:
The Chapter House

Plate 71
GLOUCESTER
Cathedral:
The Cloisters

With the Gloucester cloisters, whose oldest part dates from the years 1351 to 1377, English Gothic produced a work surpassing in beauty and ornamental richness all that had gone before, while in nobility it had no subsequent equals. The long walks have an indescribable, almost gay air about them. It is due not least to the architecture, in which the heaviness of stone seems to have been replaced by the brittle lightness of thin crystal. The walls are spun over with delicate tracery or else thinned out into glazed trellis work. There is also profuse blind tracery in the vault which is curiously atectonic. Groups of ribs spring in conoidal formations from clustered responds of reed-like slenderness. The ornamentation of these conoids gives them the appearance of elaborately cut goblets which bow towards each other and ring softly as their brims touch. The formal derivation of this kind of vaulting from the much more sober ceilings of chapter houses (plate 70) is obvious. But the structural technique is entirely different. It consists of previously prepared stone panels held together by iron brackets and not carried by a system of ribs. The mouldings which look like ribs are in fact nothing but relief decoration carved before the panels were bonded in the ceiling.

Gothic

The very word 'Gothic' as applied to architecture is a misnomer, a monument to the ignorance of seventeenth century pedants who assumed that the architecture they considered barbarous – as opposed to their own 'good Roman manner' – could have been perpetrated only by the barbarous Goths who sacked Rome. This leaves out a thousand years of history but the name has stuck and we must use it. It is not a precise word but

289

is usually applied to the architecture of the Middle Ages from the early twelfth century until the time when the Renaissance or New Learning caused, in effect, a classic revival – in the fifteenth century in Italy, in the sixteenth century on this side of the Alps.

If civilisation is the art of turning ideas and ideals into institutions then the Middle Ages in Western Europe were one of the more sublime moments in the history of man. That ideals were

Plate 72
LONDON
Westminster Abbey:
Henry VII's Chapel

The Chapel, a hall-like structure with a low ambulatory, was added to the east end of the Abbey between 1500 and 1512. It represents the end of medieval English Gothic and, as an unsurpassed – and indeed unsurpassable – triumph of decorative profusion, it is the fulfilment of the quest for ornamental effects so characteristic of English builders. The walls between the framework of vaulting shafts have become glazed trellis work with closely set, minute bars. They transform the building into a precious glass shrine permeated with light which penetrates from all sides. The vault has given up the character of a stone roof for the illusion of ethereal immateriality created by the filigree lacework of its circular patterns. As in Gloucester (plate 71), the lines making up these patterns are not weight-carrying ribs but simply tracery carved in the panelling (largely open-work) out of which are formed the pendant bosses of the vault.

A highly original feature is the springing of these pendants: they do not, as in earlier instances of this typically English vaulting device, rise from side responds towards the crown of the vault but descend from the big transverse arches, hanging freely in the air like stalactites. The original intention of the Gothic vault, to transmit through ribs to the ceiling the upward drive of vertical members, is completely denied here, indeed turned into its opposite. It seems as though the Gothic tendency to soar to heights, which

seldom lived up to alters neither the clarity of the Mediaeval system, nor the fact that its institutions were devised on an idealistic basis. Mediaeval life was based upon institutions and formulae. As the belfry chimes marked out the day from compline to vespers, so – though men worked from sunrise to sunset – did festivals and holy days mark out the year. Life itself was ordered by the Seven Deadly Sins and the Seven Sacraments. Everything was allowed for, everything systematised.

reappeared in England in the late fourteenth and fifteenth century, has been finally broken. An additional proof is the fact that the pointed arch has lost its continuously ascending flow. Known in its late form as the Tudor arch, it has depressed, almost flat curves which, in the side window of our Chapel, seem to sink under a heavy weight.

The political and class structure was rarely questioned. Even the Peasants' Revolt was a demand for existing rights, not for release from serfdom. The Feudal System might bind a man to the soil and to his master, but it established the right and duties of all men. It recognised an international aristocracy of feudal lords – fighting, ransoming, besieging each other – they called this Chivalry – but recognising each other's status, crusading together and speaking their *lingua franca* of Norman French. Their

Plate 71
GLOUCESTER
Cathedral:
The Cloisters

Plate 72
LONDON
Westminster Abbey:
Henry VII's Chapel

Plate 73
FLORENCE
Santa Croce

Although North European Gothic had reached Italy through the Cistercians by about 1200, it never struck root. To spiritualise stone, to make it instinct with living forces, was too strange a conception for Italian builders on whom Antiquity had not lost its hold. Interiors like those of the cathedrals of French or German High Gothic, soaring weightlessly to giddy heights, are not to be found in Italy, untouched as the country remained by the kind of religious fervour that found expression in these heaven-storming structures. Not that the new forms were not individually adopted: the pointed arch, the ornate capital, window tracery, even, as in Florence Cathedral, the rib vault – all these appear in Italian churches. But the way they are inserted into the whole and combined with survivals from Antiquity testifies to the continued attachment to it and to an anticipation of its rebirth.

Santa Croce in Florence, a Franciscan church begun in 1294, is not Gothic in its interior despite pointed arches in the nave arcade and windows, and the east wall. Wide and low, the nave has no upward drive; it spreads out into the aisles between the large arcades giving the whole an almost hall-like breadth against which the vertical elements make little impression. Nor is the balance altered by the pointed arches of the arcade. Counteracted by their wide span, their vertical emphasis is further opposed by the longitudinal course of powerful consoles running under the nave

architecture was the militarily scientific castle and the walled town — both common forms from the Holy Land to the Scottish Border. Their wars were dynastic and territorial, never total since it mattered not a jot to the common man whether the lilies of France or leopards of England floated over the Tower of London.

Far above the Feudal order and far above the tenuous feelings for nationalism that appeared in the fifteenth century, was the Universal Church. It may have seemed strange that Chaucer

windows. Again, the pilaster strips rising one from each arcade pillar recall Gothic vaulting shafts – but they are balked of their effect by the forceful longitudinal progress of the open roof beams. Set off by their colour, all they can do is to break up a little the sober, un-Gothic homogeneity of the wall. Taken as a whole the interior strikes one as an adaptation, not very close, of the Early Christian basilica.

should prefer English to Latin, and shocking that Joan of Arc should call herself 'French' – but the most ardent patriot would have considered the Church outside and above such controversies. There were the occasional challenges of heresy or Lollardry, but they were rare. The ideal of chastity and poverty might be unattainable, but criticism when it came was from within – the founding of yet another and even more austere monastic order, the launching of yet another crusade, the passing of even more

The impact of North European Gothic on Italy is incomparably at its strongest in the Cathedral of Milan. Begun in 1386, the church is a basilica with double aisles and a three-aisled transept and a chancel with ambulatory but no radiating chapels. The main structure was up by 1418 but finishing work dragged on until the nineteenth century. The dimensions are gigantic and the area of the interior is the largest ever attained in a Gothic church.

The exterior is faced throughout with white marble, which clothes the body of the edifice with an ornate sumptuousness that easily holds its own against the greatest achievements of the decorative art of the North. Particularly magnificent is the chancel (see plate), the oldest and most uniform part of the building. Above the sturdy, relatively high basement rises a delicately constructed fabric of stone and glass, the tracery of the vast windows being among the finest that Gothic ever produced. Pierced tracery arcades with cruciform finials embattle the walls, masking the roof behind them. From the flying buttresses pinnacles shoot up into the air making the structure bristle as though with a forest of lances. They spring from three different levels and thus form multiple lines of ascent towards the crowning lantern over the crossing.

All these individual forms as well as the structure as a whole, look remarkably un-Italian – not by accident, since numerous French and German builders were at work here. Either active themselves or as

canon laws. If the Feudal aristocracy provided a measure of patronage by castle building, it was the Church that was the great patron of the Middle Ages, one of the great patrons of history.

The myth that the monks themselves built the abbeys is ill-founded. The lay-brothers might lend a hand, the monks had other things to do. The churches were built by masons – members of their guild – under the direction of master-carvers and master-masons – men of great fame and great skill whose names – thanks

299

advisers to their Italian colleagues, they included Master Heinrich from the famous family of masons, the Parlers, and Ulrich von Ensingen, perhaps the leading German architect of his time. No doubt they were responsible for the importation of Gothic forms from the North.

to recent research – are known to us. The Church provided the money. The wealth of the Church came from many sources – from its lands and tolls, from fines in the ecclesiastical courts, from bequests and penitents, from pious kings and rich merchants. The great abbeys were built from monastic rent-rolls – almost all the Vale of Severn, for instance, was in Benedictine hands. Some of the larger and finer English parish churches were, however, built through the gifts of pious laymen – mainly the wool and cloth

Plate 73
FLORENCE
Santa Croce

Plate 74
MILAN
Cathedral

Plate 75
ORVIETO
Cathedral

Neither in the Romanesque nor the Gothic period did Italian builders adopt the use of towers to monumentalise the west fronts of their churches. The old practice, formed in the sixth century, of installing the bells in a free-standing campanile or else in a tower incorporated anywhere in the building, continued. The façade was given emphasis by other means – sculptural, or as in Orvieto, by mosaic. It became an ornate screen, no less effective in its way than the plastically differentiated, tower-crowned fronts of French and German cathedrals. Though individual forms might be borrowed from Northern Gothic, their function in the whole was entirely different. Various types of façade were evolved but they were all alike in being related to the arrangement of the interior: they presented, more or less directly, a cross-section of it. The Sienese architect Lorenzo Maitani, who designed the façade of Orvieto (1310), taking his inspiration from that of Siena (1284, by Giovanni Pisano), succeeded in expressing the interior arrangement, with its wide nave and narrower aisles. The portals with their richly-articulated surfaces and arches correspond in size to the parts of the edifice to which they severally give access, and the correspondence is repeated in the three parts of the façade surmounted by gables and flanked by slender, tower-like piers.

The overall impression is one of balance which the eye explores with equanimity. The vertical emphasis of the piers crowned with

magnates of the fifteenth and sixteenth centuries.

Out of the Church's patronage of the arts and out of her need for a great architecture there emerged another institution, neither Feudal nor ecclesiastical, free and independent, the guilds. For one who was neither aristocrat nor cleric, there was one escape from Feudal bondage – to seek refuge inside a town and there become a craftsman within a guild – free by charter. This, in the Middle Ages, even though the apprenticeship was long, was

pinnacles is countered by the horizontal band of the dwarf-gallery and the sturdy cornices with their Antique corbelling. Geometrical forms, self-subsisting and at rest — the equilateral triangle of the middle gable and the circle of the wonderful rose-window inscribed in a square — impart to the whole a calm that stills the conflict of opposing forces. In all this one can discern the pursuit of order and clarity that will soon discard Gothic ideals and return openly to the models of Antiquity. The impression is not altered by the mosaics (dating only in part from the fourteenth century) or incrustations which cover every available plain surface and are executed in bold colours against a gleaming gold ground. They enrich the façade but do not disturb its structural order.

a great incentive to craftsmanship. The guilds, being free, could impose terms upon their patrons; equally they could impose standards of workmanship upon their members. Every art and trade had its guild. The most powerful was the Masons.

Without insisting upon any cycle of the arts it does seem clear that at certain moments in history certain arts were dominant; the others were handmaidens to this central art. The classical age in Greece, because of its worship of the human form, was

306

Plate 76
VENICE
The Doges' Palace:
Palazzo Ducale

Secular town architecture, which in the fourteenth century became a distinct branch of the art, side by side with ecclesiastical building, evolved no specific type of edifice. The public buildings of the town – town-halls and arsenals – the urban residences of the nobility, the guild-halls and merchants' trading houses – all these were merely adaptations of the ordinary, artistically insignificant dwelling house as it had established itself in a given region. The only departure – and an important one – was that from the modest dimensions and general plainness of the common model. Imposing size and ennoblement by artistic means were achieved with the help of elements borrowed from ecclesiastical architecture, an indication of its continued preponderance (compare plate 77). Even the monumental Doges' Palace in Venice (built between 1309 and 1424) illustrates this process.

The broad, three-storeyed building, surrounding an inner court, derives from the type of dwelling house common in Italy but its architectural calibre raises it to the level of genuine great art. The arrangement of the exterior is entirely original. The almost unbroken, cube-like top storey seems to float over the two lower ones, transformed as these have been into pointed arch and traceried arcades. The impression that these somewhat flimsy elements will collapse

dominated by sculpture; architecture was a vehicle for the sculptor. The sixteenth century in Italy was dominated by painting, the Baroque architect striving for those sensuous or perspective and geometric effects first achieved by the painter. The Victorian age in England was dominated by literature; its stylistic revivals in architecture being purely literary – romantic or evocative. The Middle Ages were dominated by architecture. Structure was all. The other arts served architecture. Even decorative motifs in

under a crushing weight is skilfully countered by the two-colour marble facing of the top storey; the carpet-like pattern gives an appearance of extreme lightness.

sculpture, ironwork, joinery or embroidery were formalised miniature pinnacles, vaults and buttresses – a clear proof of what it was that dominated men's minds. Stained-glass and carving existed only in the service of the greater art.

That art was masonic. The functional objectives of the Medieval masons were: (a) to develop an elaborate plan – one with a multiplicity of parts but an overall unity; (b) to enclose the spaces of that plan with fireproof roofs, vaults, made from stones

Plate 75
ORVIETO
Cathedral

Plate 76
VENICE
The Doges' Palace:
Palazzo Ducale

Plate 77
LOUVAIN
Town Hall

Like most town halls of the wealthy Flemish commercial towns that of Louvain is an externally unified structure (Saalbau), with a transverse axis and several storeys. It was built between 1447 and 1463, badly damaged in World War I, then restored with meticulous respect for its original appearance. Its exuberant ornamentation marks it as a typical product of the ornamentally-minded Late Gothic. Everything that is used as decoration in contemporary church architecture seems to have been brought together here and lavishly distributed. This extraordinary richness suggests a precious shrine carved in ivory rather than a building serving secular purposes.

small enough to be carried by a pack-horse; (c) to reduce wall thickness and enlarge windows so as to let in more and more light or, rather, to provide an even larger field for the stained-glass worker, until the building – as we may still see it at Chartres – was a casket or coloured lantern; and (d) to give to the building externally a skyline, so that, seen across the woods and orchards, or above the white-walled town, the pinnacled towers should proclaim the Kingdom of God upon Earth.

313

The plan of the greater Medieval church was a consummation of centuries of development. It was highly organic – every part serving a function, all the parts related to each other. The idea of the nave, as we have seen, came to the Gothic builders from their Romanesque forerunners who, in turn, had applied their own heavy arcuated style to the simple basilican type. It was at the east end of the church that the Gothic plan grew and flowered. Projecting to north and south were the transepts – usually with

Plate 78
FLORENCE
Palazzo Vecchio

The palazzi of the Italian Renaissance, municipal buildings or stately residences of noble families, are normally grouped round a square or rectangular inner court. The earliest examples are to be found in Florence where the new architectural style originated. As in the Palazzo Vecchio, the old town hall, the inner court is laid out like the peristyle of ancient houses or the atrium of Early Christian churches. However, the colonnade supports arches and not an architrave, and the walks behind it are vaulted, not trabeated, and carry upper storeys.

The court of the Palazzo Vecchio, reconstructed in 1454 by one of the leading architects of the Early Florentine Renaissance, Michelozzo da Bartolomeo, is a very fine, and easily the most sumptuous, example of the type. One looks in vain for traces of Gothic – there are none to be found, another proof of the little appeal the Northern style had for the Italians. On the other hand motifs taken from Roman Antiquity, or at least inspired by it, abound – for instance the scrolls, festoons, masks, putti, etc. decorating the upper parts of the column shafts and recurring in the paintings inside the arcade, arranged in strips and clearly delimited sections.

chapels on their eastern wall – which became the arms of the cruciform plan. The point of intersection between nave and transepts was the 'crossing', the focal point above which there rose the flèche of the French cathedral – Paris *(plate 57)* – or the central tower of the English cathedral – Lincoln *(plate 67)*. Then again, east of this were the choir and chancel, divided from the nave by the great rood screen, making the long vista more mysterious and symbolising the difference between laity and priesthood – Amiens *(plate 60)*. This eastern limb was as long – sometimes longer – as the nave. This was specially true in the English monastic churches – as at Salisbury *(plate 68)* or Exeter *(plate 69)* – although the French made up in soaring height what they lost in the way of a long roofline.

The columned aisle of the Early Christian or Romanesque nave was, in Gothic, continued right round the chancel, behind the high altar, to form the ambulatory – as may be glimpsed in the

316

Plate 77
LOUVAIN
Town Hall

Plate 78
FLORENCE
Palazzo Vecchio

Plate 79
FLORENCE
Palazzo Rucellai

The façade of the Palazzo Rucellai shows the antique inspiration of Leon Battista Alberti, perhaps the first architect of the Florentine Renaissance to turn deliberately to Roman models. In this building he uses the system of superimposed orders as it appears particularly in ancient theatres (compare plate 12), to construct a three-storeyed framework of pilasters against the background of the wall. The pilasters articulate the wall, form clear axes, indicate, together with the cornices separating the storeys, the relationship of parts to whole, and focus the eye, which in earlier palazzi tended to slide off surfaces only horizontally divided by cornices.

view of Exeter *(plate 69)*. This ambulatory, therefore, was a complete processional way; it was also a pilgrim route, the shrine of the saint – St Thomas of Canterbury, Edward the Confessor at Westminster, St Cuthbert at Durham and so on – being immediately behind the altar. Again, opening eastwards from the ambulatory, was the Lady Chapel or, as at Westminster, Henry VII's Chapel – mausoleum of kings *(plate 72)*. In England the eastern limb and the Lady Chapel were usually, not always, square-ended; in France they were polygonal, thus giving the opportunity for that chevet of radiating chapels, as at Rheims *(plate 58)*.

The Gothic builder took the Roman and Romanesque vault to its logical conclusion .... and beyond. Noble and monumental though vaults such as Vézelay *(plate 44)* or Caen *(plate 48)* might be, they had severe limitations. Like the big vaults of the Roman Thermae they were based on the semi-circular arch. The Romans, as has been said, got rid of much massive walling, concentrated

322

Plate 80
ROME
The Capitol:
Palazzo dei Conservatori

Begun about 1546, and therefore chronologically still part of the High Renaissance, the palace is so clearly an anticipation of Baroque that one feels entitled to consider its author, Michelangelo, as the 'father of Baroque' – not only in painting and sculpture but in architecture as well. Comparison with the façade of Palazzo Rucellai in Florence (plate 79) brings out the forward-looking features of our building. Alberti had divided his façade into a series of equal fields framed by pilasters and moulding.

The storeys are laid evenly on top of each other; the particular character of the lowest storey with its entrances is to a large extent masked by the distribution, uniform throughout, of the pilasters. Calm and balance are the dominant characteristics, and they will remain so in the palaces of the mainly Roman High Renaissance, even though achieved by other, more plastic means. Michelangelo's structure departs from this type in many ways. Its two storeys are not evenly balanced. The lower has become a colonnaded walk with an architrave, and as such it is completely dominated by the higher. At the same time the division of the storeys, clearly marked in the Palazzo Rucellai, is here abandoned for a compelling unity brought about by huge pilasters carried from ground to cornice. These enormous vertical members, known as the giant order, which appear here for the first time and so may well have been an invention of Michelangelo's, were to become a favourite Baroque motif. Used

thrust at a few points and let in more light – all by means of the cross-vault, two intersecting half-cylinders. They set out their building in square bays – each bay opening out into the next – and on each side of each bay was a semi-circular arch. If the tops of those intersecting vaults were to be level with each other, then clearly the arches on all four sides of the bay must all rise to the same height. Since those arches were semi-circular each bay must be a square on plan.

both as columns and as pilasters they served to give the function of supporting and carrying weight an exaggeratedly emotional expression (see plate 95).

Besides, it is precisely from this façade that the derivation of the giant order can best be understood. If the regularly distributed pilasters and the entablature they carry are considered by themselves, they immediately recall the peristyles of ancient temples.

In a large and simple hall, such as the Thermae or even a Romanesque nave, this did not matter. The whole building could be planned quite simply as a series of squares – on the basis of what we would call a square module. But the moment the plan has to respond to the requirements of mediaeval ritual, it becomes much more complex and the square becomes inhibiting. The tyranny of the square bay is seen at Angoulême *(plate 45)* where the whole church is planned on the over-rigid basis of two square

324

Plate 79
FLORENCE
Palazzo Rucellai

Plate 80
ROME
The Capitol:
Palazzo dei Conservatori

Andrea Palladio, the designer of this palace, built between 1550 and 1557, one of his many works in Vicenza, was the leading architect of the late Renaissance. He identified himself to a greater degree than any of his predecessors or contemporaries with the tradition of Antiquity, making his own the rules of Vitruvius, the art theorist of the time of the Emperor Augustus. He developed his theories in his Four Books on Architecture, *a programmatic treatise which had a lasting influence, especially in France and England (see plates 92, 97, 107).*

In the Palazzo Chiericati the colonnades and entablatures of the two storeys meticulously follow Roman models. However, in spite of its rigorous classicism, the building as a whole is on the borderline of Baroque. While the effects of volume and the clear separation of the storeys are Renaissance features, the emphasised middle portion of the façade suggests the Baroque predilection for structures dominated by their centres. The pedestals on the cornice carrying statues and vase-like forms are on the axes of the columns and bring to flower, as it were, the sap rising in them − another anticipation of the Baroque.

bays of the aisle to one square bay of the nave. This is still true at Durham − just as Gothic is about to be born. When we have polygonal East-ends, ambulatories, radiating chapels and octagonal chapter houses, the system of the square bay collapses. If the arches on all sides of a rectangular or irregular bay are all to rise to the same height then the pointed arch − slightly pointed over wide spans, steeply over short ones − is the solution.

The pointed arch is the key to Gothic. In the high vaults,

therefore, at St Denis, Chartres or Durham, Gothic may almost be said to have been invented. The whole of the heavy architecture of Romanesque was immediately liberated, emancipated, and the way was open for continuous development over three hundred years .... from the first Gothic glories of the twelfth century cathedrals of the Ile de France to the Chapels Royal of Tudor England *(plates 56 to 72)*.

The Gothic builders, like the Romanesque, tried to reduce the

Plate 82
ROME
St Peter's (Dome)

The church architecture of the High Renaissance found its spatial ideal in the centrally planned building, developed evenly on every side, unorientated, and focussed in the crowning dome. The longitudinal structure used almost exclusively in the Early Renaissance gave way before the centralised one which was to achieve its climax in the new St Peter's at Rome. It was Pope Nicholas V (1447–1455) who decided that a new church should be raised after repeated attempts had shown that the old and venerable Constantinian Basilica was beyond repair. After a series of delays work began in earnest in 1506, under the direction of Donato Bramante whose design provided for a Greek cross surmounted by an enormous dome. However, at his death in 1514 only the walls and the piers for supporting the dome had been erected. Raphael, who was next put in charge, toyed with the idea of adding a nave, but his successor, Antonio da San Gallo, reverted to Bramante's plan. In 1547 the building was taken over by Michelangelo, then over seventy, who modified considerably the original design, especially that of the dome. Bramante, inspired perhaps by the Pantheon (plate 11), had planned a hemisphere on a low drum, a form agreeable to the High Renaissance because it focusses and brings to rest the lines of force rising from the central space below, thus imparting to the interior the serenity of a whole reflected on itself. As against this conception, Michelangelo mounted his dome on a

amount of wooden centring used during construction. The ringed or compound Romanesque arch, with its corresponding compound pier below it, was carried still further. The simple rings of the Romanesque arch became an elaborate arrangement of mouldings as, for instance, at Cologne *(plate 61)*, Salisbury *(plate 68)* or Exeter *(plate 69)*. Indeed one aspect of the history of Gothic lies in the changes that these carved mouldings underwent. The familiar terms used to describe the phases of English Gothic

high drum (the latter executed by himself, the cupola after his design by Giacomo della Porta between 1588 and 1590), gave it a steep curvature, almost that of a pointed arch, and directed the movement expressed in the coupled pilasters of the drum along broad ribs up to the shaft of light in the crowning lantern where it loses itself in the infinite distance of a painted heaven – a break with the finite repose which the High Renaissance had sought and found in its spherical domes, and a step towards the strainings of the Baroque.

However, in the end St Peter's did become a longitudinal church. Carlo Maderna, responsible also for the monumental façade (plate 93), began in 1607 to extend the unfinished eastern wing of the central structure into a powerful, barrel-vaulted nave. This departure from the ideal of space pursued by the High Renaissance cannot be accounted for in practical terms alone: what had been built so far did not cover the whole site of the Constantinian Basilica and thus left vacant consecrated ground. The wish not to allow any of it to become desecrated may have carried some weight in the decision to extend the church lengthwise, but the general change in architectural style which occurred in the middle of the century made the decision in any case an easy one to take. Under the influence of the militant religiosity of the Counter-Reformation the longitudinal plan, better suited for ritual purposes, became again dominant.

– 'Early English', 'Decorated' and 'Perpendicular' – were a Victorian invention and cannot be given any specific dates or be taken too literally. 'Early English', however, is an austere thirteenth century style in which the mouldings are simple and unadorned, the arches steeply pointed, the whole style a reaction against the heaviness and round arches of Romanesque. Salisbury (AD 1220) is the supreme type. 'Decorated', as its name implies, is rich, more ornate and representative of the Chaucerian Age

Plate 81
VICENZA
Palazzo Chiericati

Plate 82
ROME
St. Peter's (Dome)

Plate 83
ROME
Il Gesù

Under the impact of the Counter-Reformation, church architecture takes a new direction from the middle of the sixteenth century onwards. Militant religiosity and a new emphasis on otherworldliness could not express themselves adequately in the ideal of the High Renaissance, the centrally planned church which, equal on all sides and serenely pointing nowhere but to itself, was neither well adapted to the requirements of Catholic liturgy nor yet convenient for an exposition in eloquent symbolism of the mysteries of the beyond. In Late Renaissance architecture, therefore, the horizontally emphasized longitudinal scheme, better suited to these needs, was again taken up. However, this was not a simple return to the Early Renaissance type, akin to the Early Christian basilica, colonnaded, flat-roofed and flowing continuously from entrance to chancel. Creations of the Renaissance itself, inspired by ancient Roman models, were drawn upon, the longitudinal barrel-vaulted hall resting on piers and the centrally planned domical structure. Il Gesù in Rome, built for the Jesuits by Vignola and Giacomo della Porta between 1568 and 1584, and to become the model of many Baroque churches, shows a combination of these two diametrically opposed schemes. The combination is not new: already Sant' Andrea at Mantua (after 1472, from Alberti's design) had been given – exactly as here – a barrel-vaulted nave flanked by aisles transformed into a series of chapels, and a domed crossing.

and of Merry England. Exeter Choir is a good example, while outside England we have Strasbourg *(plate 63)* or Ulm *(plate 64)*. After the Black Death the whole Gothic style was impoverished or, at any rate, simplified. Ornament was reduced to mere 'Perpendicular' panelling until, with a return to richness late in the fourteenth century, this panelled style – wherein the mullions and transoms of the windows are, so to speak, carried across the wall-face – 'Perpendicular' blossomed into the Indian Summer

337

But Il Gesù goes significantly beyond this possible model in that the domed space is not, as at Mantua, a centre holding together the surrounding spatial units but the goal in the movement of the interior. To achieve this effect the depth of the transept and therewith the emphasis of its transversal direction have been considerably reduced, and the nave and chancel given a subdued lighting, while a flood of light streams through the dome which rises like a luminous apparition from the surrounding penumbra. Thus an element has been drawn into the articulation of space that will play a great role in Baroque architecture: light – as a source of tense oppositions and complicated optical effects.

Il Gesù announces the Baroque in other respects as well. The articulation of the nave walls, the aisles divided into a series of chapels that have little spatial contribution to make, the low balconied galleries (coretti) above the chapels, the small clerestory windows cutting into the vault with their lunettes – all these will appear, with variations, in Early Baroque churches.

of Gothic as we see it in, say, the fan-vault of Gloucester cloisters *(plate 71)* or the intricate and lace-like pendant vault of Henry VII's Chapel *(plate 72)*.

These phases of Gothic were all reflected in the crowning glory of the style – the vault. The Roman vault had had a smooth and unbroken under-surface; during construction a complete 'reverse' of the vault had to be made in wood. The Romanesque builder, however, constructed a series of arches both across the vault and

338

Plate 84
BLOIS
Château:
The Great Stair

The first reception of the Italian Renaissance in France occurs already in the fifteenth century. When in 1495 Charles VIII (1483–1498) went to Naples on a military expedition to secure his hereditary rights, he and his suite were so impressed by the magnificent churches and palaces of Italy that he summoned Italian artists to France, both to build and to train native architects in the new art. Louis XII and, above all, the artistically-minded Francis I (1515–1547) continued Charles' efforts. However, in France as in other countries north of the Alps, the Renaissance had to wage a long struggle with medieval tenets and practices, and at least until the end of Francis I's reign, the old and the new continue to appear side by side, often in curious and very attractive combinations.

The Château of Blois, on the Loire, is laid out irregularly round an inner court with various parts ranging from the thirteenth to the seventeenth century. Francis I enlarged it about 1520, adding a powerful wing of several storeys on the north side, which offers a fine example of this 'transitional' style. Of particular interest is the great stair on the court side. While the floors in Italian palazzi usually communicate internally and by a straight stair, Blois keeps to the old external and spiral Gothic type. It has balconies between projecting piers from which the court could watch tournaments. In structural and decorative detail old and new intermingle. Thus the piers are fashioned as Corinthian pilasters and their

along its groin or diagonal, as at Caen *(plate 48)* or Laon *(plate 49)*. This framework or 'lobster pot' of arches or – as we must now call them – vaulting ribs, needed centring only for the ribs themselves. Once these were built it was comparatively easy to bridge stones across from rib to rib in the form of "infilling". Both ribs and infilling are clearly seen in the foreground of the view of Bourges *(plate 59)*.

It was soon discovered that the more ribs there were the easier

pedestals carry typically Renaissance grotesque ornament. The balcony balustrades recall Gothic traceried parapets but the lowest has balusters all'antica, *and the two higher one are filled with the emblem of Francis I, the crowned salamander. Of Gothic derivation also are the gargoyles and the figures standing under canopies, the latter covered with Renaissance decoration. In general the predilection for exuberant ornament and bizarre effects, at its strongest in the crowning entablature, is part of the Gothic legacy.*

it was to build the infilling. Moreover, as the number of ribs increased – and there are fifteen springing from each capital at Exeter *(plate 69)* – it was realised that the Gothic vault, a highly functional roof, could also be a very decorative ceiling. Purely decorative ribs began to appear, while the points where the moulded ribs crossed each other, being difficult to handle smoothly, were left as knobs of stone – then carved as the boss. Thus did a whole system of decoration grow out of a solution of the roofing

340

Plate 83
ROME
Il Gesù

Plate 84
BLOIS
Château:
The Great Stair

Plate 85
CHAMBORD
Château

problem. The story of Gothic is largely the story of how the masons mastered each step in this development of the vault. There was the problem of setting out the curve of each rib on the workshop floor, of cutting each moulded voussoir for its place in that rib, of making all the ribs grow smoothly and organically from their common springing point on the capital. The vault of Henry VII's Chapel *(plate 72)* merely shows the limits, some would say excess, to which the art of the medieval

town, along the 'streets' of the terrace, the roof becomes a fairy-
tale landscape of intermingled shapes. This fanciful treatment of
the roof is a Gothic inheritance; the adjacent parts of the buildings
are also affected by it. Decorative detail, on the other hand, and
the articulation of the body of the building with pilasters and cornices
stamp it as a work of the Early Renaissance.

mason could be taken.

Along with the development of the vault went the development of the window. The vault could develop not only as its
technique was mastered; it depended also upon the related problem
of thrust, of the buttress and flying-buttress – Paris *(plate 57)*.
When this problem too was solved, then in effect the wall had
vanished. Only the point of support remained; the mass of the
wall had been absorbed into the buttress. This, though in stone,

Plate 86
PARIS
The Louvre:
Pavillon d'Horloge

This magnificent structure is the work of Jacques Le Mercier (1585–1654), the initiator of Early Baroque in France. It dates from about 1624, so that chronologically too it belongs to the Baroque. However, it may suitably be considered in connection with the Renaissance because, except for modifications in the top storey and roof, Le Mercier closely followed the design of Pierre Lescot, and added the Pavillon d'Horloge to the west side of the Louvre quadrangle which Lescot had not only planned but executed (begun in 1546) – in the style of the fully developed French Renaissance. This accounts for the curious combination of a clear, classically inspired system of articulating pilasters and engaged columns with a tendency to enrich the wall surface with all kinds of figure decoration, trophies and so on. The tendency is characteristic of the French High Renaissance which, in contrast to the Italian, was not content with the classical balance and perspicuous disposition of columns and cornices but used sculptural effects to achieve greater sumptuousness.

was what a modern engineer has in mind, in terms of steel, when he speaks of 'point loading'. This was always the aim of the Gothic builder – to pare away the wall, let in light, and provide more and more scope for the stained-glass worker. So, in Henry VII's Chapel *(plate 72)* or at Milan *(plate 74)* we see the windows running almost from buttress to buttress. The 'lantern church' had been achieved.

The large medieval window, however, was not at all the same

347

thing as the large modern window. The object of the latter is to provide a big area of unbroken transparency. The object of the former was to provide a rich grill to be filled with coloured glass. Plate glass, anyway, was not available. There also had to be resistance to wind pressure, while in scale and texture the moulded mullions and window arch had to echo the vault above. Hence the tracery window, divided and sub-divided by its stone bars or mullions; hence the rich patterns of that tracery as the bars

Plate 86
PARIS
The Louvre:
Pavillon d'Horloge

Plate 87
MUNICH
St. Michael

While most of the churches, municipal buildings and castles built in Germany in the sixteenth century share with similar structures of the period in France, the Low Countries or England, the dualism of old and new, Gothic and Rennaissance, St Michael in Munich (1583–1597 by Wolfgang Miller and Friedrich Sustris) shows a unity of design that can stand comparison with contemporary Italian works.

This is exceptional but not accidental: the church was built for the Jesuits, and Miller, who was the first architect, deliberately took Il Gesù (plate 83), dedicated in 1584, as his model. The nave, spanned by a wide barrel vault, is flanked by recesses as in Il Gesù; but there is no dome to let in a stream of light and the low tribunes above the chapels are also missing – two important features which the German Baroque will take up.

The hall-like nave is lit through windows sunk in deep recesses and not visible from the entrance. The source of light thus appears indirect and the eye is not distracted. This, together with the absence of a dome and the emphasis on the chancel as the point of convergence – achieved by narrowing it in relation to the nave and giving it a bold fenestration – lends to the interior a compactness lacking in the Roman model. At the same time the lack of colour results in a sober yet solemn atmosphere; it is not mellowed in any considerable way by the sculptural enrichment of the walls and, in

intertwine to fit themselves under the arch – Rheims *(plate 58),* Strasbourg *(plate 63)* and Milan *(plate 74).* Thus once again, as with the arcades and the vault, out of a practical solution of a practical problem there emerged an art form, an architecture.

Thus could one continue the analysis down to small details or to humble village churches, even the manors, cottages and barns. When architecture is the dominant art of an age, then, inevitably, it takes on the likeness of that age. The Middle Ages were a most

comparison with the splendour of Il Gesù, has a somewhat chilling
effect (it must be borne in mind, however, that the ornamentation
of Il Gesù is not original but dates from the seventeenth century).

intricate system of institutions and concepts – the material and the ideal never far apart. And both the age and its architecture were absolutely logical if we grant the transcendental basis of it all. It was an age and an architecture which gave poetic solutions to real problems.

354

Plate 88
HEIDELBERG
Castle:
Ott-Heinrichs Bau

Among the castles built by German reigning princes in the six-teenth century, mostly in the towns where they lived, Heidelberg ranks highest in artistic merit. It consists of a series of extensions of the thirteenth-century stronghold, of which the one begun in 1556 for the Elector Palatine Otto Heinrich is the most important. It was modelled on the palazzi of the Italian Renaissance – witness its broad front of three storeys raised on a sub-structure and divided into tiers by sturdy cornices, and the articulation with pilasters and half-columns. But of the Italian clarity of disposition, and reduction to essentials, little has remained; on the contrary, the façade is largely covered by a wealth of ornament of various kinds leaving practically no free wall surface which in Italy always predominates. The Ionic pilasters of the first storey do not have ordinary shafts but are made up of bands of ashlars with deeply incised joints. Those of the second storey, Corinthian, are filled with grotesque ornament. Moreover, the columns in all three storeys alternate with niches sheltering statues, which obscures the tectonic relationship between carriers and carried by deflecting the pilasters and half-columns from their role of articulating supports into that of frames for the large windows. The mullions of these are in the shape of hermae *supporting the entablatures. The windows in the first storey are surmounted by triangular gables with angels carrying medallions, while those in the second and third have*

Renaissance

John Ruskin called Venice 'a golden clasp upon the girdle of the earth'. Because of its place in the geography of a Europe still gathered about the Mediterranean, Venice in the years of her greatness was a focal point. If the arcades of the Doge's Palace *(plate 76)* do not quite demonstrate the structural dynamic of the Gothic North, they do show us some of the richest Gothic of all. In the domes of St Mark's – those great golden caverns – we

355

above them instead of the gable a bizarre ornament, partly figures,
partly abstract motifs.
In fact, the façade of the Ott-Heinrichs-Bau is treated primarily
as a carrier of ornament and not as a surface on which to project
the structural relationships of the whole. This, together with certain
other characteristics, suggests that the architect in charge, whose
name is not known, was a Netherlander.

have the essence of Byzantium, as far west as it ever came; while
in Longhena's great dome of Salute we have, equally, the essence
of Baroque, as far east as it ever came. But Venice is unique.

By and large the soil of Italy was unsympathetic to Gothic.
The towers and pinnacles, the vigour of the high vaults and buttresses belong to the grey North. There is only one Gothic church
in Rome, and some Italian Gothic – as for instance Orvieto
(plate 75), with its mosaics and marbles, is strangely un-Gothic.

356

Plate 87
MUNICH
St. Michael

Plate 88
HEIDELBERG
Castle:
Ott-Heinrichs Bau

Plate 89
AUGSBURG
The Arsenal

At the turn of the seventeenth century a reaction began in Germany against the luxuriance of ornament, well exemplified in the Ott-Heinrichs-Bau at Heidelberg (plate 88). St Michael's Church in Munich (plate 87) and a number of municipal buildings erected in this period show a programmatic acceptance of the classical lucidity of the Italian Renaissance. Among them is the Arsenal at Augsburg, built by Elias Holl between 1602 and 1607. The articulation of the façade is at first sight a surprise because its threefold vertical division and particularly the sturdy volutes flanking the gable at the top are quite obviously taken from Italian churches. But whatever may have prompted this remarkable borrowing, the glance towards Italy had a fortunate effect on Holl's work. The façade reads easily, the function of the ground-floor as a socle is appropriately brought out, and the structural relationship between the vertical members and the cornices separating the storeys convincingly presented. Yet the building is shot through with an unclassical restlessness. It has a pronounced vertical emphasis and the movement conveyed in the pilasters seems to have such momentum that it imperils the stability not only of the top triangular gable but even of the window mouldings. This charging of the mass of the structure with an imaginary force is a bold anticipation of

The cathedral at Milan *(plate 74)* is nearer to the real thing but, standing as it does almost beneath the Alps, is a northern building and, in Italy, almost a freak. Such Gothic structures as the nave of Florence cathedral or of Sta Croce in the same city *(plate 73)* are notable more for their large Roman scale — four bays of the nave at Florence equal fourteen at Westminster Abbey — than for any real understanding of Gothic principles.

The Medieval system had been developed in the North. The

the Baroque which is also foreshadowed in the stronger three dimensional contrasts obtained, for instance, by the doubling and trebling of the pilaster shafts.

system of thrust and counter-thrust had been hammered out mainly by the master-masons of central France – the Ile de France, significantly the heart of Feudalism. During those centuries Italy had slept; the popes had been in exile at Avignon, the emperors at Byzantium; the Imperial ruins had been quarried and had decayed, while sheep grazed in the Forum and Rome sank into insignificance. Meanwhile all through Europe a new mercantilism, a simple form of capitalism, had been coming into being to replace

Plate 90
ANTWERP
Town Hall

As in France and Germany so in the Low Countries the ideals and forms of the Italian Renaissance ousted traditional notions only very gradually. From 1540 onwards an attempt was made with some success in what is now Belgium, to integrate the sensibility of Late Gothic and the lucid regularity of the new Italian architecture.

The Town Hall of Antwerp built between 1561 and 1564 by Cornelius Floris de Vriendt, is a good example of this development. With the generous breadth of a palazzo, with Tuscan and Ionic orders rising successively above a rusticated basement, with horizontal divisions by cornices modelled on Antique entablatures, the building has a distinctly 'Italian' air about it. But entirely autochtonous is the idea of breaking up the façade by a powerful, gabled central member that challenges by its vertical emphasis the prevailing horizontality. One is immediately reminded of the Gothic Cloth Hall in Ypres whose low, broad front is similarly divided by a high tower in the middle.

the purely ecclesiastical rule, the almost purely subsistence economy, of the thirteenth century. The later parish churches of England had been built with lay and mercantile wealth. At Florence, where the silver Arno wound between purple hills, the great Medici family had, in the fifteenth century, lifted themselves into being the world's first large-scale international bankers. We call it banking, the Middle Ages called it usury, and – while there could never have been a Reformation in Italy – this first assertion of secular wealth, with all its attendant arts and luxuries, did not go unchallenged.

The conflict between the austere monk, Savonarola, and the rich Florentine merchants, symbolised even in the Catholic South the first birth pangs of secular power as against ecclesiastical. Patronage was shifting slowly from bishops to princes; art was to be henceforth aristocratic – neither a peasant craft nor monastic. That conflict, though limited and localised in Florence, was, north

Plate 89
AUGSBURG
The Arsenal

Plate 90
ANTWERP
Town Hall

Plate 91
HATFIELD
Hatfield House

On the continent the sixteenth century, dominated in the sphere of ideas by Humanism and the Reformation and in that of art by the Renaissance, marks a sharp break with the medieval past. England, however, was enabled by her geographical isolation to develop both politically and culturally in a more peaceful and continuous manner. In particular, the history of English architecture at this time seems to illustrate the abiding national trait of respect for tradition. A limited interest in the creations of the Renaissance appears first in the culturally vigorous reign of Elizabeth (1558–1603) but on the whole, up to the beginning of the seventeenth century the last flowering of Gothic, the Tudor style, elaborated at the turn of the sixteenth, remains dominant. Borrowings from the Renaissance do occur but only as isolated bits of 'new fangled' finery added for decorative effect to traditionally built structures.

Hatfield House, built between 1607 and 1611, stands at the end of this period. It is one of the numerous country seats that the English nobility had begun to build for themselves under Elizabeth. Its extended plan – a centre piece and wings – is in marked contrast with the compactness of Italian palazzi and French castles (see plate 85), but is typical of the English Early Renaissance. It answers the desire for picturesque effects and creates a variety of angles for delightful views of the park and the landscape beyond. Characteristic and still entirely Tudor is the treatment of the two

of the Alps, to be nothing less than the Reformation itself, then the Wars of Religion. That same conflict, as we see it in England a hundred years later than in Florence, was the conflict between Church and Crown, between Henry VIII and Wolsey. In the Reformation countries, however, the change in patronage was more complete. Elizabeth of England built no churches, her courtiers built only gorgeous palaces, whereas in Italy church and palace building went on side by side. In Italy the change was

projecting wings. Their corners are emphasised by small square towers, while the contrast between the red brick of the body and the light freestone of the tower edges, cornices and window frames is attractive. Traditional features are the concealed roof, the upper edge of the wall softened by the traceried balustrade (it could also be a crenellation), the surface of the wall vertically articulated by equal windows above each other and large bay windows with a trellis of small lights running from the ground through the main storeys.

Against the conservative wings the centre piece shows in its façade a stronger influence of the Continental Renaissance. Built entirely of freestone and provided with pilasters, columns and other Renaissance motifs, it strikes both in colour and structure an aesthetically satisfying and historically interesting contrast. It shows that while the old will continue to be preserved the new can now also be received.

mainly stylistic; in France and England it was the basic art form itself that changed.

In 1453 the Turks sacked Constantinople. Byzantine refugees, bringing with them ancient manuscripts and classical traditions, reached Florence. This Renaissance seed there fell on fertile soil. Basking in Medicean wealth the 'New Learning' and the new fashions that went with it flourished. There, in a land that had never forgotten its classical heritage, and with the ruins of the

Inigo Jones (1573–1652), who built the Banqueting House between 1619 and 1622 as part of a gigantic palatial group of buildings which he planned but did not execute, was the leading architect of what in England corresponds to the High Renaissance (roughly 1625 to 1665).

He went to Italy twice for long periods, studied principally the works of Palladio, became an enthusiastic advocate of the Italian's teaching, and successfully transplanted the new style to England, in the face of conservative opposition. In the design of the Banqueting House he closely follows his revered master among whose works the Palazzo Chiericati in Vicenza (plate 81) suggests itself as an obvious comparison.

The comparison is all the more instructive as it shows that, strictly though he adheres to the Palladian regularity, in the last resort Inigo Jones builds as an Englishman. Palladio uses strong plastic contrasts, organises his structure round the clearly emphasised centre, differentiates his storeys by varying their height according to their relative tectonic importance and masks the top of the building with figure pedestals. Jones gives his building a flat compactness, crowns it with the clear horizontal of a balustrade, makes the storeys, raised on a rusticated basement, of equal height and hints at rather than makes explicit the special role of the centre portion by providing it with three-quarter columns as against

Roman Empire all around, the 'New Learning' was, in effect, a revolution in thought; it initiated a more civilised, more refined more lavish way of life …. at least for a few. The secular and aristocratic arts – the palace and villa and all that went with them in the way of costume, jewelry, painting, furniture and gardens – became a dominant art form. The professional artist, trained in the Renaissance workshop, might be poet, painter, sculptor; he was also expert in the 'orders' and canons laid down

pilasters on the sides. In all this one can discern, even if slightly modified, certain typical traits of English architecture to be observed already in Romanesque and Gothic structures, tendency to distribute similar members and units evenly and to articulate the wall with a sparing use of the third dimension, by linear rather than plastic means.

by Vitruvius. His emergence brought to an end the long reign of the master-mason.

Immediately, therefore, we have a new phenomenon in European architecture – the architect. As opposed to traditional mason or craftsman, the architect instructs others how to build; he works through the drawing-board rather than on the site ; he is primarily a scholar with a knowledge of the antique. At his best he might be a superb although always, in a sense, a second-hand master;

Plate 92
LONDON
The Banqueting House
Whitehall

Plate 93
ROME
St. Peter's and Piazza

The transition from Renaissance architecture to Baroque – in Italy it occurs in the last decades of the sixteenth century, and first in Rome – is not marked by nearly so radical a break with the past as that from Gothic to Renaissance had been. On the contrary, the Baroque develops organically out of the Renaissance. It is a logical consequence of the earlier style and not conceivable without it. But, close and manifold as the relations between the two styles, at least initially, may have been, their respective products differ essentially. True, the Baroque takes over to a large extent the methods of construction and the repertory of architectural motifs elaborated by the Renaissance but its aesthetic postulates and principles of composition are different. While the masters of the Renaissance in its late phase, immediately preceding the Baroque, Palladio, Serlio and Vignola, model themselves on the antique ideal of rigour and regularity, the Baroque breaks away from the principle of following a precedent and seeks to invent on its own. It manipulates the available stock of motifs without much regard for the canon of Antiquity and, where the Renaissance had sought clear and static disposition, a harmonious balance of forces and the serenity of tensions resolved, the Baroque produces sudden contrasts, complicated optical impressions and rhetorically exaggerated conflicts of opposing forces.

All these tendencies have left their mark on the grandiose façade of St Peter's erected in 1612 by Carlo Maderna, one of the leading architects of the Early Baroque in Rome. Gigantic supports rivet

at his worst he was a dilettante pandering to fashion. All this does not mean that the buildings of the Renaissance were 'copies' of Greek or Roman models – that came only in the nineteenth century – but that they did make use of a classical vocabulary. The Renaissance building was composed of classic elements – the Doric, Ionic and Corinthian 'orders', cornices, balustrades, pediments etc. Also, the well-ordered, balanced and symmetrical plan was restored to architecture. This classical vocabulary became

377

the lower storeys to one another and prop themselves in a Herculean stance against the sturdy mass of the entablature and the high attic. Equally characteristic for the Baroque is the pronounced emphasis on the centre of the façade. Projecting slightly from the rest of the structure and marked off by the concentration of the gigantic order and the flat triangular pediment, it imposes its domination on the whole even though the flanking bell-towers preserve a distinct autonomy. Both the emphasis on the centre and these side accents with the tension they create spring from the Baroque predilection, constantly in evidence, for a grouping of masses about points of gravity to achieve visually exciting effects of volume. (Compare Michelangelo's Palazzo dei Conservatori, plate 80, to appreciate the change from Renaissance to Baroque.)

Maderna's façade became the monumental termination of a vast piazza given its present world-famous appearance by an architect of genius, Gianlorenzo Bernini. He enclosed it, between 1656 and 1663, in a sumptuous colonnade, characteristically for the Baroque oval in shape. This attempt to create an external setting for the edifice, to isolate it from the crowd of houses in the midst of which medieval churches used to be erected, to give it command over large open spaces and thus relate it to the outside world in a way commensurate with its significance, embodies an important Baroque postulate, that of treating the free space in which a building is erected as an integral part of the architectural design.

universal throughout Europe in the centuries that followed.

An architectural vocabulary, however, must always be applied to current building types; it must always take account of current needs, of building methods, of climate and of taste. Style alone is not architecture and, in architecture at any rate, history never repeats itself. In Medicean Florence we have, for example, great stone-faced palaces, looking inwards upon a courtyard but built right up to the street line and foreshadowing the big classic banks

A feature of the Baroque particularly common in Italy is the architectural treatment of open squares in their own right. The favourite element employed is the fountain. It is rare, however, that it should be treated as a real building to the same degree as the magnificent Fontana Trevi, erected by Niccolo Salvi probably from a design by Bernini, and completed in 1762. Here, architecture, released from the task of enclosing an interior, is free to form a delightful alliance with sculpture. The sturdy façade of the palazzo which supplies the background seems to grow out of the bizarre undulations of the unhewn rock over which fall gently murmuring, thread-like cascades, under which winged horses and tritons play. The large figure of Neptune turns to them with an imperious gesture as though to command peace. The god is the centre of the whole scene: the mass of rocks rises towards him and the architectural framework – a typical product of the fully developed Baroque with its striking sculptural accents, powerful columns and pilasters, and bold cornice projections – converges on the tall recess in front of which he stands.

of modern cities. Such palaces – as well as churches – were a requirement of the age. The Pitti, Strozzi, Riccardi and Rucellai were Florentine examples; the Farnese and Giraud were Roman ones. There was no real precedent for them in ancient times.

The architects of the early Renaissance, particularly Brunelleschi in Florence, and Alberti – who wrote about theories of proportion – adapted their classical vocabulary to what were then modern needs. They used their classical detail with skill and

379

restraint. The Palazzo Vecchio in Florence *(plate 78)* shows, it is true, some of the richness of this strange Medicean episode, but in Alberti's Palazzo Rucellai *(plate 79)* we see the flat, elegant, almost Greek purity of the design – the pilasters, rustication and ornament being little more than a surface texture, the only bold feature being the crowning cornice, typical of all Florentine palaces.

Ideas in those days travelled slowly and it was a couple of

Plate 93
ROME
St. Peter's and Piazza

Plate 94
ROME
The Trevi Fountain

Plate 95
TURIN
Superga

The late phase of the Italian Baroque brought with it a reaction against the arbitrary, often capriciously overdone, atectonic inventions which characterise the works, akin to the German Rococo, of Borromini, Guarini and others. Rigour of form and lucidity, adherence to rules and a measured monumentality were again emphasised, as they had been in the Late Renaissance with its gaze fixed on Antiquity.

Perhaps the first to return to the precepts of Palladio and his time was Filippo Juvarra, the leading architect of the Italian Late Baroque. His most important work, the Superga outside Turin (built between 1717 and 1731), an imposing overture to an extensive monastic group of buildings, does not, it is true, quite succeed in breaking with the Baroque. The tendency to rhetorical overstatement is still present in its gigantic features. But the simplicity and lucid design recalling an ancient temple, of the colonnaded portico, the clear composition of the domed central rotunda, and the neat distinctness of the various components suggest the discipline of a classical ideal. The distance travelled from High Baroque can be measured by comparing the dome with the finicky bell towers over the wings which in a curiously conservative way have preserved the rich, playfully elegant forms of the previous period.

generations before the Renaissance conception of art and life could cross the Alps to France and to England. Then the French armies of Charles VIII, leaving behind their gabled and belfried towns, marched over into Lombardy, there to discover a new world. They returned in excitement, with books about art, and with artists – Leonardo da Vinci was one of them – in the king's train.

The chateaux of the Loire Valley were the first expression of the Renaissance in France. Machiavelli's conception of 'The Prince' was exemplified in Francis I, the Renaissance idea of life in the costumes, gaiety, richness, immorality and cruelty of his Court. The hunting boxes of the Loire – built for king and courtiers – show both the extravagance and limitations of the Renaissance on the unsympathetic soil of Gothic lands. These chateaux show none of the symmetry, classic restraint or elegance of Florentine palaces. They are romantic extravaganzas. They

386

Plate 96
VERSAILLES
Palacc

The magnificence, self-glorification and love of display of the absolute monarchs of the late seventeenth and early eighteenth century is embodied in their enormous palaces. Just as Louis XIV (1643–1715), le Roi Soleil, *became the archetype of the absolute prince, imitated by every ruler in Europe, so his palace in Versailles established itself as the much admired and often imitated model (especially in German Baroque palaces) of the royal residence. Louis XIII had had a hunting lodge built in Versailles (begun in 1624), laid out as a horseshoe round the so-called* Cour d'honneur. *In his successor's vast structure, begun in 1668 by Louis Le Vau and continued from 1678 onwards by Jules Hardouin Mansart, extensive wings were added (length from end to end 629 yards), and the original horseshoe enclosed in a larger one. The central portion of this, facing the garden (see plate), became the celebrated* Galerie des Glaces. *It presents an imposing front, whose lucid and compact design points to a derivation from Italian palazzi but at the same time testifies to the measured classicism of French Baroque (of which the* Dôme des Invalides, *see plate 97, is the chief witness).*

The vast building does not shut itself off from its surroundings but on the contrary subjects them to the plenitude of its absolute power. The large park, one and a quarter of a mile long, is cut by avenues,

are, in essence, mediaeval castles – Blois *(plate 84)* and Chambord *(plate 85)*. Chambord was a huge castle with bastions, outworks, round towers and a moat – almost a garrison town in itself. It was begun in 1519. Where does it differ, then, from the purely military castle of the previous century? It has large and spacious rooms for entertaining; it has big windows looking outwards upon a relatively secure world; it has a moat which is really an ornamental water; its walls have lavished upon them – though

387

striking into it like rays of power from the palace, while its water
basins, fountains and innumerable bronze and marble statuary provide
a festive setting for the architecture.

all misunderstood by the craftsmen – surface ornament and arabesque based upon pictures in Italian pattern books. The gorgeous nature of the Court was symbolised in the skyline. It was like huge plumes blossoming in a hat. The conglomeration of turrets, minarets, pinnacles, chimneys and dormers, seen far off in the hunting forest, gave us one of the most fantastic skylines in history. How little the word 'style' can mean is shown by the fact that in the history books the Palazzo Rucellai and Chambord

Plate 95
TURIN
Superga

Plate 96
VERSAILLES
Palace

Plate 97
PARIS
Les Invalides

French Baroque is characterised from the outset by a clear, measured classicism. True, it practises the common Baroque effects of emphasised volume and size but it avoids confused overstatement, aiming at serenity and monumental greatness, products not of the emotions but of abstract reason acting according to rule. Thus its works are in many respects akin to those of a Palladio or to the classicizing edifices of a Juvarra (plate 94).

The Dôme des Invalides in Paris, built between 1680 and 1706 by Jules Hardouin Mansart is perhaps the best example of this cool rationality. The exterior of the structure – built on a Greek cross plan and domed – is dominated by the contrast between two compact, clearly delimited masses: the horizontally emphasised two-storeyed, square basement with a façade articulated in the manner of an ancient temple, and the vaulted rotunda rising from it. The balance of the whole and the almost academic rigour of the arrangement of the orders speak for themselves.

are both dubbed 'Renaissance' .... merely because both use the classical 'orders'.

In Elizabethan England, a generation later, the situation was not unlike that in France. The Queen herself built little; her rich courtiers and merchants used the wealth of the New World – which in rivalry with Spain they exploited so ruthlessly – to express both their own pride and ostentation and their own cult of sovereignty. Drama and poetry, rather than architecture,

393

might now be the dominant art, but something of the intricate craftsmanship that had once built Henry VII's Chapel or King's College Chapel, now went not only into an Elizabethan sonnet, but also into the building of country mansions only a little less fantastic than those on the Loire. Once again, Renaissance or classical architecture is misunderstood; this is not surprising for, after all, the builders of Hatfield, Longleat or Kirby had never been to Italy. At Hatfield *(plate 91)*, for instance, we see how

While in Italy the Baroque reached its finest flower, while France and England moved from Late Renaissance to Early Baroque, the ravages of the Thirty Years' War (1618–1648) turned Germany (which may, for our purposes, include Austria) into an artistic desert. Beginnings of Baroque architecture, as they appear for instance in the works of Elias Holl (plate 89) led nowhere. General stagnation prevailed long after the Peace of Westphalia and when, in the last third of the seventeenth century, building began to increase, foreign architects had to be called in because war and decay had destroyed the links with native tradition. In the Protestant North builders from the Netherlands are the most numerous, in the Catholic South, Italians. Only at the turn of the century do German architects appear, and from about 1720 onwards they are in the majority.

These German architects were pressed into service by an enthusiasm for building equally shared by clergy, princes, nobility and burghers, and without parallel even in the Gothic period. Palaces and houses of God became the two dominant items in a programme to which was added, linking the two as it were, monastic architecture. This began to flourish under the patronage not of the young orders, the Jesuits for instance, but the Benedictines, Premonstratensians and Cistercians, the patrons, that is, of its earlier, medieval apogee. Ambitious, and in open competition with the palaces of the temporal and spiritual princes, they abandoned the traditional layout round a cloister reflecting the monastic withdrawal from the world. Instead

the classical 'orders' are piled one on top of another to make an ornate 'frontispiece' in the centre of the house. The house itself, however, for – all its spacious planning – is virtually a mediaeval manor of plain brick with mullions and leaded lights. 'Style', the Italian Renaissance, is found only in a few trappings. Here, unlike Italy, the professional architect is still a rare bird. While he might supply the fashionable Italianate detail, the general structure was, as it had always been, a matter that was left to

they raised vast complexes with living quarters, libraries, schools, guest rooms and so on, out of all proportion with the number of resident monks, decorating them both inside and outside with an exuberant splendour which seemed a total denial of monastic simplicity and austerity.

Were it not for the presence of a church building these monasteries could easily be mistaken for secular palaces. The church façade is treated as a centre for the other buildings, with which it is aligned. The wings extend far to the sides and are grouped round courts behind the church. The sites chosen are no longer hidden, out of the way places but localities distinguished by the beauty of landscape and capable of setting off buildings to advantage.

All this found its perhaps finest realisation in the Benedictine Abbey of Melk, designed mainly by Jakob Prandtauer (the church was built between 1702 and 1738). The vast structure (about 350 yards long) rests proudly on a rock plateau dominating a large tract of landscape. The effect of the West front (see plate) is incomparable. Flanked by the extremities of the monastic buildings and girt by the semi-oval of the picturesquely curved terrace with a balcony-like opening in the centre, the two towers of the façade rise as it were from the rock over the Danube. The structural variety, particularly the undulating walls and entablature of the façade, the double pilasters and the complicated spires, is characteristic of the rapidly matured, individual style of the German Baroque.

the country builder.

It was only in James I's reign that the real professional architect, fully responsible not only for ornament but for the total form of the building, appears in the English scene. As a designer of scenery and costumes for Court masques Inigo Jones had won favour, but it was only after he had been to Italy and returned with a full sketch-book that he won his title of 'father of English architecture'. In the Queen's House, Greenwich, and then, in

396

Plate 97
PARIS
Les Invalides

Plate 98
MELK an der DONAU
Benedictine Abbey

Buried in the solitude of the rocky valley of the Danube not far from Ratisbon lies the Benedictine monastery of Weltenburg. Its church, built between 1717 and 1721 by the brothers Cosmas Damian and Egid Quirin Asam, is one of the most impressive and most mature achievements of South German Baroque. While the exterior is sober and simple, the splendour inside is so overwhelming and spell-binding that the experience of it can be hardly rendered in words. Architecture, sculpture, ornament, colour, and light have contributed to create an interior that partakes of a miraculous reality and makes it possible to understand why such works have sometimes been called the 'Throne Halls of God'.

The entrance leads first into a small, oval domed space, a kind of vestibule, whose sparely lit darkness invites one not to tarry but to proceed further into the liberating luminosity of the main interior (see plate). Here the intensity of form and colour – the large and eloquently powerful structural members, the glistening gold of the ornament and the stucco reliefs – at first suggests the ceremonial hall of a palace rather than a place intended for devotion and prayer. But this impression of profaneness is quickly and wonderfully transformed into one of religious awe. The columns and entablatures carry a domical superstructure with a large opening in the middle through which the shell of a second dome is visible. This higher dome seems to lose itself in the infinity of heaven: the ceiling fresco by Cosmas Damian Asam representing the Virgin interceding before

1619, in the Banqueting House in Whitehall *(plate 92)* – intended as part of a larger palace – he gives us the 'real thing', the anglicized Italian palazzo façade. He scaled it down, adapted it to the English climate. In doing this he showed himself the first Englishman to understand what classicism and the Renaissance really meant. In a city of gables and narrow alleys the Banqueting House must have stood out as a startling modern building.

Thus we see how in Italy, France and England the Renaissance

Christ in the midst of mountainous clouds and hosts of exulting angels masks the materiality of the vault with an illusion of heaven. The illusion is convincing because the supports of the vault are concealed and the painted heaven floats weightlessly in mid-air like an ethereal apparition. The supernatural effect is completed by the light: it pours in through invisible windows, lends a mysterious semblance of luminosity to the paintings themselves and thus makes them appear as the source of light for the space below which, windowless, receives no light except this heavenly one and, with it, heavenly consecration.

The chancel, further to the east, is transfigured into a similar miracle of light. Against a background of blinding luminosity, again from an invisible source, a figure of St George in gleaming silver armour, transfixing the dragon with his lance, rides into the penumbra of the altar zone. Fantastic side screens with vine columns recalling the flats of Baroque stage design form the frame of this fairy-tale performance, while the Queen of Heaven appears between angels against golden rays emitted by a sun-like apparition. All this shows to what extent Baroque architects were influenced by the theatre, which in this period rises to great cultural importance, indeed becomes almost an element of life itself. Here, however, its possibilities are used not to distract but to make the divine apprehensible to the senses; to focus the mind on the higher world.

had its birth. It was primarily an Italian thing and it was in the great Italian cities that it advanced to become the basis of all European architecture, both under the name 'Renaissance' and, in its more mature form, as 'Baroque'. As such it became an architecture less universal than Gothic, more aristocratic, but for all that the only architectural language Europe had throughout the seventeenth and eighteenth centuries.

402

Plate *100*
EINSIEDELN
Abbey Church

While Italy reverts after 1700 to a certain classicism, discarding the fanciful, floating compositions of its High Baroque, as they had been developed in particular by Borromini and Guarini, for the greater rigour, clarity and calm of an Antique inspiration (plate 95), Austria and even more South Germany take this Baroque, introduced from Italy in the seventeenth century, to extremes. The works of Borromini and Guarini, especially their churches, with their flowing and overlapping interiors, sinuous walls and mouldings, sumptuous ornament and paintings glowing with colour, do not by any means lack movement, variety or opulence. But they are as nothing compared with what was produced from the same premises north of the Alps. As though unshackled by any rules, the creative fancy of the architects reaches into ever new dimensions, inventing more and more complicated spatial compositions that astonish and bewilder by their constant changes of direction and their dancing movement. It is rare to find so much spatial clarity remaining as there is at Weltenburg (plate 99). Usually one is confronted by a succession of architectural puzzles all the more insoluble because even relatively simple parts of the interior are decorated with such an exuberance of form and colour that the structural framework cannot be divined.

As in the Abbey Church of Einsiedeln in Switzerland (1721–1725, by Kaspar Moosbrugger), in which a nave of three domed bays

Baroque

A generation ago the word 'Baroque' was a derogatory term. It was reserved wholly for what were then considered the more extravagant, ornate and violently sculptural manifestations of classicism, mainly for the palaces or churches of the old Austrian Empire, of Bavaria or Spain. It now has a wider connotation. It includes almost all architecture which uses the classic vocabulary except the first pristine Renaissance, except the Palladian Revival,

leads to a longitudinal chancel, the visitor is bewildered and intoxicated by the abundance of decoration. Every surface is covered by stuccoed ornament, capitals and cornices seem to froth and quiver. Bunches of flowers, foliage and fillets are scattered over the arches, and in this opulence, which the glittering gold and glowing colour raise to the intensity of a Dionysian revel, angels and putti flutter about. They act as links with the paintings in the vaults which with their painted cornices draw the side walls into the ceiling and thus receive them into the infinite spaces of a higher world filled with holy figures. The presence of these paintings gives its deeper meaning to the festive splendour of the whole: the over-powering chorus of rejoicing in which architecture, sculpture, stucco and painting join together, becomes a prelude to the experience of the glory of God and Heaven.

and except, of course, the *neo-Grec* of the nineteenth century.

It is difficult to measure the influence upon architecture of painting and sculpture. It is difficult to say how much architectural form responded to town-planning – to the desire, for instance, to create the dramatic skyline of the royal capital – whether Rome or Vienna, or the little towns of German princelings. All these things played their part. A great master, such as Michelangelo – equally a sculptor, painter and architect –

Plate 99
WELTENBURG
Monastic Church

Plate 100
EINSIEDELN
Abbey Church

Plate 101
SWABIAN ALPS
The Pilgrimage Church
'In der Wies':
The Chancel

With the Church 'in the Meadow', built by Dominikus Zimmermann between 1746 and 1754 in a lonely meadow of the Swabian Alps, German Church Baroque celebrated one of its finest but also one of its last triumphs. The exterior, sober and unpretentious, as is usual in this period, offers no hint of the miraculous metamorphoses inside. Again architecture, sculpture, painting and ornament have produced a composition which in its luminous, decorously rejoicing gladness, seems to echo the sounds of Mozart's music. Especially the longitudinal chancel, into which flows the elongated oval of the nave, is arranged in a way that almost forces the comparison with the floating lightness of a minuet and the delicate notes of the harpsichord.

The chancel has a gallery the effect of which is to give the columns and arches a 'lining' of light transforming them from space-articulating elements into the supports of a floating baldachin. The light fulfils its task wonderfully. It caresses the bodies of the columns, brings to flower the pastel blues and red-browns of the stucco marble, studs the gilding of the balustrade trellises, the capitals, and the foliage with scintillations, trickles through the sinuously curved openings under the vault, and brings out from the colour-impregnated shadows by the altar the white figures of saints in ecstasy, gambolling putti, and flying angels. It plays over the curdled foam of the rocaille which in a restless movement licks

undoubtedly allowed one art to influence another. His mastery of three-dimensional form, of the geometry of the human body, his mastery of the plastic and the sensuous – as we see them in his gigantic sculptures – certainly influenced the equivalent forms in the mighty figures of his Last Judgement, or that combination of grace and strength that we see on the Sistine ceiling .... and then all that in turn influenced the size and rotundity of domes, columns or great moulded plinths. A painter's love and knowledge

the edges of the painted heaven. No stillness, no firm boundaries to hold the eye; only exciting, complicated dance movements in a fantastic setting to which the weight of stone and the laws of statics seem to be foreign.

of perspective, a sculptor's mastery of the plastic, could hardly fail in combining to influence his architecture.

Baroque architecture had freed itself from classical discipline. The classical vocabulary – column, cornice, pediment, steps etc. – remains in the service of the Baroque, but the architect feels within him the power to use these elements with freedom and for the creation of something fresh – virtually of a new architecture. Baroque architecture is not really sculptural in the sense

Plate 102
VIERZEHN-
HEILIGEN
Pilgrimage Church

Baroque church façades, like those of earlier periods, were the centres of interest in the articulation of the exterior. Here the architect displayed the wealth of his repertory and here was the place for the picturesque effects so dear to the Baroque. The purpose now as before was to emphasise the importance of the entrance side, to provide a solemn introduction to the rest of the building. Two basic types of façade established themselves: that introduced by Il Gesù in Rome and adopted by its Italian followers – a towerless screen with a sturdy pedimented centre portion and low side pieces; and the two-tower front more in line with native tradition, of which Vierzehnheiligen (1743–1772, by Johann Balthasar Neumann) is an example. The renderings of these types vary from church to church, but the articulation whether rich or sober always follows the same principles as those applied to interiors. There is the same multiplicity and complication of visual effects; features are added which are not structurally required; cornices project boldly, pediments are broken (as here in Vierzehnheiligen) and curiously atectonic shapes delight the eye by their alternate recessions and juttings out. And, a feature of particular significance, the wall of the façade is no longer flat. It is charged, as it were, by secret forces which swell and bulge its surface in various directions and give an undulating movement to cornices and gables as though these were not of stone but of some pliable material.

that Greek architecture was sculptural – for it is only incidentally a vehicle for sculpture. Nor is Baroque a carved architecture as was Gothic, in the sense that carving emphasised the lines of life or of structure. Sculpture and painting are now, in seventeenth century Europe, the dominant arts; architecture responds to them rather than governs them. Great vistas and scenic effects not only serve the aristocratic idea; they are the stock in trade of the painter. The extravagance of Baroque lies in the attempt to turn

411

The façade of Vierzehnheiligen has all these characteristics though with them it combines a noble, eminently satisfying reserve. It lacks the extreme opulence of other German façades of the period.

them into a reality. They become part of Baroque as may be seen in domes and avenues, piazzas and squares and palaces set in parks. Equally, however, Baroque is also sculptural in the sense that the main forms of the building itself are now modelled – curved, twisted, piled up – almost as if the architect were modelling not the ornament on the building but the building itself.... instead of constructing it. Construction is always necessary, but whereas Gothic glories in it, Baroque defies it.

412

Plate 102
VIERZEHN-
HEILIGEN
Pilgrimage Church

Plate 103
WURZBURG
Palace: The Residenz

The secular architecture of the German Baroque found its main scope in the palaces of the princes. Germany offered wide possibilities to both native and foreign architects, for its approximately 350 temporal and spiritual rulers saw in lavishly extravagant architecture a setting for elaborate court ceremonial and the best way of satisfying their absolutist aspirations. The canon had been established by Versailles (plate 96), that symbol of absolute monarchy, and the various German potentates, great and small, sought to apply it as literally as they could.

Not least among them was Johann-Philipp, Prince-Bishop of Würzburg and a member of the family of the Schönborns who seem to have been possessed by a veritable mania for building. The size and appointment of his palace, begun in 1719 by Johann Balthasar Neumann, are worthy of royalty. The three wings are grouped after the French model round a court (cour d'honneur) which opens out into a wide square. The back of the palace which looks out on a garden delightfully varied by fountains, waterfalls, steps, orangeries, and arboured walks, is treated as one unit. It is emphasised at the extremities by flat projections, and dominated by the richly articulated centre which is brought forward as one large bay. With its bulging mezzanine and the picturesque curves of its roof it sets up a vigorous central accent typical of the German Late Baroque, ever in pursuit of enlivening effects. Also characteristic

Baroque can be, but is not necessarily, richly ornamented. The colonnades enclosing the Piazza of St Peter's in Rome *(plates 82, 83 and 93)* are one of the great achievements of Baroque. They are unornamented and they use the most austere form of the Doric order. Their Baroque character lies wholly in the fact that the colonnades themselves are curved, that the masses of the building, not just its parts, are as if modelled. The colonnades are swung round by Bernini – a sculptor before he was an

417

is the accumulation of sculptural elements: like the sinuously curved window gables and the ornate window frames which recall those of Baroque pictures.

architect – in order, first, to enclose a vast and highly dramatic elliptical piazza, and, second, to set off Michaelangelo's dome and the west front. Both objectives are typically Baroque. They are achieved by typically Baroque means. Sculpture does not serve the art of architecture by being applied to it; architecture has here taken to itself some of the attributes of sculpture.

It is the essence of Baroque that it does not, like Gothic, marry itself to the landscape. It imposes itself and makes its own

Plate *104*
BRUHL
The Augustusburg:
The Staircase

The staircases of Baroque palaces were among the finest and most imaginative creations of the architects of the period with their sense of spatial effects as expressions of courtly magnificence. Staircases were usually decorated as opulently as the large ceremonial halls in the palace, and nearly always surpassed these in the variety of architectural invention. Their practical purpose offered inspiration in that they not only enclosed space with four walls and a ceiling but also rose in it from level to level. The simplest solution, that of connecting the various floors by one unbroken flight of stairs, would have been as unsatisfying to Baroque architects as a stair tower or flights confined in narrow passages. For the function of the staircase as they conceived it was not merely to connect floors but also to provide a fitting approach to the splendour of the main rooms and a setting for elegant display. Hence the hall-like spaciousness and stately flights which ascend in different directions.

As an example we illustrate the staircase of the Augustusburg in Brühl, built between 1744 and 1748 by Johann Balthasar Neumann, and among the most mature and most magnificent Baroque creations of this kind.

landscape, urban or rural. Gothic is a natural architecture; Baroque is an artificial one, glorying in its power to handle these huge columns and these great flights of steps. In Baroque man flatters himself and his institutions. In, say, the Palace and Park at Versailles *(plate 96)* we see how the whole concept of royalty and of absolutism can, by means of Baroque, be imposed and stamped, as if by a seal, upon the French landscape.

The Baroque dome, as we see it in St Peter's *(plate 93)*, in

419

Les Invalides, Paris *(plate 97)* or in St. Paul's, London *(plate 106)*, typifies the whole Baroque attitude to structure. We saw in the case of the Pantheon *(plate 11)* how the ancient Romans built their largest dome with almost brutal directness. The space it covered was circular; the walls were thick and well piled up round the base of the dome at the point of maximum thrust; the apex of the dome was made as light as possible by being actually cut away to make a central 'eye'. All these basic points in dome

Plate 104
BRUHL
The Augustusburg:
The Staircase

Plate 105
DRESDEN
The Zwinger:
The Gate Pavilion

Of the gigantic palace, that the 'most Baroque' of European princes, Augustus the Strong, Elector of Saxony and King of Poland, intended to build in Dresden, only the so-called Zwinger was completed (1711–1722, by Mathäus Daniel Pöppelmann). A square court was enclosed by galleries, serving as orangeries, and emphasised by larger hall-like structures at the angles. It was intended not only as an approach to the palace but also as a setting for the plays and spectacles so popular with the pleasure-loving Baroque rulers and courtiers. Seen in this light, it is a translation into stone of what were elsewhere temporary wooden stands, intended for spectators. However, more interesting for our purposes than the function of the buildings is the arrangement of the pavilion-like gate-houses designed to accommodate the courtier-spectators.

Higher than the adjacent galleries, the pavilions outstrip them – as indeed everything else that the inventive German Baroque has to show by way of complicated forms – in the multiplicity of ornament. Unfortunately the very characteristic and well-known Central Pavilion (Wallpavillon) has not yet been fully restored after suffering damage in the last war and could not be photographed. But the Gate Pavilion illustrated, with its accumulation of structurally unnecessary columns and pilasters, its broken pediments, bizarre coats of arms, masks, vases and figures, shows well enough of what fantastic, purely gratuitous 'theatre' this late phase was capable.

building were ignored by Baroque architects. The Baroque dome is poised on pendentives which carry it over the central area of a great cruciform church. The Baroque dome – so that it may be not merely a roof but a dominant in the city's skyline – is raised up on a drum far above the point where it might get abutment from surrounding building. The Baroque dome – again for the sake of skyline – is topped by a cupola at just that very point where it should be relieved of weight. In the generally large scale upon which Baroque builders worked this cupola may be quite big — that of St Paul's, for instance, weighs some 800 tons. Thus does Baroque defy structure for the sake of effect. All manner of devices must be resorted to in order to carry the cupola. In the case of St Paul's it is borne aloft by a huge brick cone, concealed by the outer dome. Again, the dome itself, lacking all abutment, must somehow be prevented from bursting outwards. The only answer is to chain it in at the base. No less than seven chains are embedded

426

Plate 106
LONDON
St. Paul's Cathedral

Throughout the period of the Baroque and into the eighteenth century, English architects continued to practise almost exclusively the Palladian clarity and rigour of form imported from Italy by Inigo Jones (see plate 92). The style was well suited to the sober, practical English mind, and Inigo Jones may be said to have laid down a binding law when he commented that 'in architecture ye outward ornaments oft (ought) to be sollid, proporsionable according to rulles, masculine and unaffected', and that 'composed ornaments . . . do not well in sollid Architecture'. True, the entirely different notions of the Italian High Baroque did not remain unknown, and Inigo Jones' first and greatest successor in the line of royal architects, Sir Christopher Wren, was fully conversant with them when he planned the new St Paul's to replace the Gothic structure destroyed in the Great Fire of 1666. But in the end the more traditional and typically English, functional attitude to architecture prevailed and in the gigantic structure, erected in one effort between 1675 and 1710, the remarkably ornate pinnacles of the towers and the dome are practically the only element recalling the creations of the contemporary Italian Baroque. Otherwise the whole exterior – and the interior – is articulated with rigorous clarity.

It is significant that in Wren's design too the specifically English features, which we have repeatedly noted, are strongly in evidence.

in the masonry of St Peter's dome. It is all highly scenic. Baroque regards structure as its servant, resorting to shifts and subterfuges providing always that the ultimate effect is achieved.

Once this principle is accepted then the way is open for the use of almost any sensuous, plastic, fluid or flamboyant shape. So we have Baroque in its ultimate and freest form – the Baroque of Austria, Bavaria or Spain. In some of these monastic churches, such as Melk *(plate 98)* or Einsiedeln *(plate 100)* we see the style's

Suffice it here to mention the predilection for monotonous alignments of identical features. It is exemplified in the two orders of the façade in which the twin pairs of columns carrying heavy entablatures are separated by equal distances, and the presence of the portal at the back of a vestibule behind the lower order is just hinted at by a slightly wider space between the central columns. The drum of the dome shows the same principle in all its purity. It is encircled by a gallery with an evenly spaced colonnade and the motif is repeated in the flat by the pilasters articulating the attica above.

structural aud sculptural limits. Or, as in the palaces at Würzburg *(plate 103)*, Brühl *(plate 104)* or Dresden *(plate 105)* we have just very charming and very skilful confections. For the sake of these all the illogicalities and exesses of Baroque are easily forgiven.

Plate 105
DRESDEN
The Zwinger:
The Gate Pavilion

Plate 106
LONDON
St. Paul's Cathedral

Plate *107*
HAMPTON COURT
Palace

This view of Hampton Court shows the Privy Garden and Park fronts (1688–1698). Sir Christopher Wren planned an almost complete reconstruction of the Palace, recalling the Louvre which he had seen on his visit to France in 1665, but this plan was never carried out. In fact only part of the Palace was rebuilt, and in an altogether simpler and more English style. The skyline is flat and unbroken, the plan, excepting the slightly projecting wings of the Privy Garden front, perfectly rectangular. The regularity of the white stone windows against red brick is only broken by inconspicuous centrepieces. This makes the façade almost austere, and, like the sixteenth century Hatfield House (plate 91), exemplifies the persistence of linearism in English architecture.

Plate *108*
SANTIAGO DE
COMPOSTELA
Cathedral

Outside Germany the Late Baroque was nowhere so fanciful and opulent as in Spain. But the Spanish version was entirely different from the German: instead of complicated spatial compositions, undulating dancing forms or a joyful Bacchanalian exuberance in decorative detail, we find an accumulation of architectural ornament unparallelled in its intensity. However much the works of the masters of the period, Churriguera, Vasquez and others, may differ among themselves, they have all in common a certain overheated, exotic

Stylistic Revivals

There the straightforward story of European Architecture might end, were it not that between the Baroque and our own Modern Movement there lies that most curious revival of the historic styles. In the nineteenth century almost every architect was an accomplished eclectic, prepared to work in almost any style. The Classic and the Gothic Revivals are merely the most outstanding. Partly the result of greater historical knowledge, partly the result of the

433

luxuriance of invention. A particularly fine example is the façade
(begun in 1738) which Casas y Novoa added to the old and
venerable Romanesque Cathedral of Santiago de Compostela
(compare the façade of Vierzehnheiligen, plate 102).

complete collapse of craftsmanship in face of machine production, partly the result of professional snobbery, these stylistic revivals monopolised the architectural field during the greater part of the nineteenth century. Perhaps they were due even more to the Romantic Movement. Romanticism is the divine discontent of the artist, the flight from an all too sordid present – sordid industrialism – to all that is charming, distant or strange in an idealised past. In nineteenth century England the dominant art was literature.

Plate 107

HAMPTON COURT
Palace

Plate 108
SANTIAGO DE
COMPOSTELA
Cathedral

This imposing structure is a major example of the Neoclassical style, which appeared in England and on the continent in the late eighteenth century. The British Museum was begun in 1823, but the distinctive façade, with its largely correct Ionic details, was probably not decided on until the 1830's. It is the most impressive work remaining by the architect Sir Robert Smirke. The many columns of the design are characteristic of the period, and similarities can be seen in the work of Smirke's German contemporary Schinkel. Architects throughout Europe continued to practise the style throughout the first half of the nineteenth century.

Both the ancient and the medieval world came to be seen through a golden haze – induced by the poets, by the novelists and by the no less literary pre-Raphaelite painters. The prosperous commercial cities usually found the best expression of their wealth and dignity in Roman or *neo-Grec* town halls. Romantics, eccentrics and Tractarians found their expression in Gothic Revival churches – and the Victorian age was one of church building. This Battle of the Styles was fought out between architects with surprising

439

bitterness, while the real building achievement of the Railway Age was engineering. Both styles, however heterodox and eccentric though they might seem in their early days, came to be officially accepted. The British Museum, for instance *(plate 109)*, with its huge Ionic peristyle, is a fair example of *neo-Grec*. The Houses of Parliament *(plate 110)*, with its towers and pinnacles and mullions – though it concealed within its romantic exterior a most efficient and un-medieval plan – set the seal of official approval

440

The nineteenth century produced no architectural style of its own. Its originality consisted in reviving the styles of the past. Scholarly interest in the cultural heritage of Antiquity, particularly Greek Antiquity, had contributed to the rise of Neoclassicism which took its models from this heritage. With the Romantic Movement the Middle Ages came culturally into their own, and medieval architecture began to be studied and imitated. England, where Romanticism originated and where Gothic had never been quite forgotten, was the first to stage a Gothic Revival. Her example was followed on the Continent especially in Germany.

The finest product of the Gothic Revival in England is the gigantic Houses of Parliament (1840–1852, by Sir Charles Barry). The rich effect of the façade owes much to the work of Augustus Pugin, Barry's assistant, who designed the strictly Late Gothic details (Perpendicular; compare plate 72). Its use for so important a building imposed neo-Gothic as more or less the national style in architecture.

upon the Gothic Revival. It was probably the greatest single architectural monument of the nineteenth century.

Plate 109
LONDON
The British Museum

Plate 110
LONDON
Houses of Parliament

Plate 111
DRESDEN
Opera House

In the thirties of the nineteenth century the disciplines of Neo-classicism went out of fashion. In the historical panorama of styles the next to find favour was the richer, livelier style of the Italian Renaissance. Gottfried Semper's Dresden Opera House (completed 1841; burnt down, and rebuilt 1871–8) struck the decisive blow for the new style in Germany. Semper modified his first influential design in the building illustrated here, but it is no less decidedly Italian in style. The impressive entrance, the clearly organised plan (which owes something to Semper's plans 1865–7 for a projected Munich Opera House), and the well-defined composition of the exterior mark it out as an important example of the Renaissance revival.

Plate 112
PARIS
Opera House

The procession of revived styles continues: after the revival of the High Renaissance comes that of the Baroque. The works produced by this movement, often characterised by a vainglorious braggadocio, are rare. A very typical example is the Opera House in Paris (1861–1874), designed by Charles Garnier. This is the best-known building of the Second Empire, for which the contemporary Place de l'Opéra provides a suitable setting. The luxurious decorations of the interior are matched by elaborate exterior details, including a sculptural group by Carpeaux. An imposing colonnade and the central half-dome of the auditorium make the main contributions to an impressive neo-Baroque effect.

Plate III
DRESDEN
Opera House

Plate 112
PARIS
Opera House

INDEX

The *plate* numbers of the illustrations are given in bold type, followed immediately by the *page* numbers (distinguished by asterisks) on which the descriptive notes relating to the plates are to be found. All other references are to matter in the text and notes.

453

458

460